The Wheelsmen

by
Ric Mixter

Updated August 2012

www.lakefury.com

Dedicated to
those who led me to storytelling-
My parents Richard & Alice
(who bought me my first typewriter and tape recorder)
and
Fifth grade teacher Gordon Rice
(the greatest teacher ever)
and
High School teacher Jim Dellies
(who let me use his ELECTRIC typewriter!)

cover photography by David A. Sommers

Copyright © 2009 by Airworthy Productions, Saginaw, MI
No part of this book may be reproduced in any manner whatsoever
without written permission from the publisher.
Published by Airworthy Productions- www.airworthy.tv
Printed in the United States of America
First Printing 2009
ISBN-13 978-0-615-33540-7

The Wheelsmen

FOREWORD

I've been fortunate in my travels to meet and interview literally hundreds of people. Most of these encounters were from behind a television camera, working for news stations around Michigan. I left TV news to go into industrial videography, but found I was still fascinated by the stories, interviewing people about recruitment and safety rather than the typical news fare of car accidents and strikes. I decided to try documentaries to satisfy my craving for story telling and I was soon staring at library microfiche screens all around the Midwest. This is where I would first learn of the sailors' stories. There were several good books about Great Lakes history, but all lacked a personal story from the gale. I was also surprised to learn that there were no documentaries on Great Lakes stories. This would be my calling, and with an estimated six thousand shipwreck stories to tell, I knew I had to narrow down my scope.

I had become interested in shipwrecks when one occurred on my 'beat.' I was paged to respond with my camera to the Saginaw River in Bay City where the fuel tanker *Jupiter* had exploded. I spent the night on the scene as the tanker burned and we were called back during breakfast when the ship rekindled. Only days later I was walking its melted deck and I was instantly hooked on shipwreck stories. This was the largest tanker disaster ever on the lakes and I wanted to know more. I managed to get the TV station to pay for diving lessons and I borrowed a special underwater camera to film the wrecks near Alpena, Michigan. The series took first place honors with the Michigan Association of Broadcasting and I became hooked on swimming these underwater museums.

But I needed more than to see the weathered bones of a long-lost schooner or the the rusted metal chunks that remained from a steel freighter. I yearned to know about the storms that raged during the fall and I wanted to hear these stories first hand. Reading the faded newspaper accounts was no longer sufficient, so I used the newly formed internet to start tracking down survivors.

I found that local newspapers did a lot of the work for me, as reporters spotlighted survivors every time a major anniversary rolled around. That's how I found Ed Kanaby. He was a rare look at the 'king of storms;' an eyewitness to the last moments of several steel ships that were lost when the winds raged at 60 miles per hour for sixteen hours straight. His story would become my first TV documentary and the beginning of my partnership with David Norris and Dan Hall. This song-writing duo would transform my long-winded interviews into incredible verse, further setting my course for creating unique maritime documentaries.

Today it's been fourteen years since Mr. Kanaby passed and I now have amassed interviews from several storms and shipwrecks. Many of these men have also passed on, leaving these video images as the only 'full' story to what they saw. My effort was to go beyond the short news 'quotes' found in newspapers to document rare glimpses into the *person*.

I also note that of the dozen or so survivors I have chatted with over the years, the majority were at the helm when the ship was lost. I have no idea why this is so, but I do know these men were in a unique place in history. From the wheelhouse, they provide an unbiased scrutiny of the events that took their ships, beyond the corporate line usually towed by the captain or mates. Each man was 'at the wheel' when their ship was lost. They are the wheelsmen.

The Wheelsmen:

Edward Kanaby sailed the steamer *H.B. Hawgood* into a weekend of devastation in November of 1913. The gales would become known as the "King of Storms" because of the destruction caused on the lakes. Giant steel vessels simply vanished in the tempest, taking 250 sailors with them. Chapter one explains how the crew of the *Hawgood* managed to escape disaster, thanks to a wheelsman who disobeyed his captain's orders to head back out to sea.

Lloyd Belcher was at the wheel during what many believe to be the most powerful lake storm ever. The Armistice Day Storm of 1940 raged with 126 mile per hour winds, sinking three freighters and two fish tugs. Lloyd and the crew of the Canadian steamer *Novadoc* would be rescued by three local fishermen who dared to venture out to where the Coast Guard would not. Lloyd would return to sailing after the killer storm, only to be bombed by the Nazis during the invasion at Normandy.

Ray O'Malley was aboard the Coast Guard cutter *Escanaba* when it mysteriously exploded near Greenland during World War II. The *Esky* was well known as a lifesaver, famous for rescuing over 100 survivors of the torpedoed troop transport *Dorchester* in 1942. Ironically, it would be the *Escanaba's* crew in need of rescue only a few months later. The survivors were found floating on a broken spar in the frigid North Atlantic.

Len Gabrysiak was steering the *Cedarville* when it was lost in 1965. The captain ordered full steam ahead into fog so thick that you couldn't see the entire length of the ship. A tragic collision took ten men almost instantly, but Len still suffers from the accident today.

Steamship *H.B. Hawgood*

Ed Kanaby wheelsman of the steamer *H.B. Hawgood*

Chapter One: "Not While I'm a Wheelsman"

Edward Kanaby was born on September 4th, 1895 to Charles and Anna Kanaby. Charles had recently immigrated from Germany; his wife, the former Anna Lemanski, was from Poland. They carved out a small farm in Harbor Beach, Michigan, and with Ed they now had four able farmhands. There is no doubt that Edward watched the ships that would make port at Harbor Beach, because by age 16, he left home and found work aboard a steamship. Starting out as a deckhand, he quickly worked his way up to the pilothouse and was soon under the employ of the Acme Transit Company of Cleveland.

Ed was assigned to the *H.B. Hawgood*. Four hundred feet long, the *Hawgood* certainly would be a giant compared to early freighters, but when it was launched in 1903, there were ships coming out almost 100 feet longer. It was certainly something to steer, and at eighteen years of age, Ed Kanaby was certainly considered young to be working in the wheelhouse. As fate would have it, another wheelsman had left the ship and the captain did not have many choices to replace him, so Kanaby went from watchman to wheeling, and his trial season would certainly put his skills to the test.

By early fall, the *Hawgood's* crew was looking forward to the winter break, with only a handful of scheduled trips remaining. On November 9th they sailed the empty freighter up the St. Clair River to pick up a cargo of grain on Lake Superior. It was a long run to Northern Ontario, creeping up the lakes at just over ten miles an hour.

Meteorologists knew something was brewing when they tracked two separate areas of low pressure advancing through Canada and in the southern half of the United States. Southwest winds increased in speed on Friday, November 7th and storm flags were raised to warn those who were still in port. Those ships that were already underway were out of luck. Very few Great Lakes freighters had the luxury of wireless telegraphy, with the majority of new fangled 'radios' aboard only passenger ships and car ferries.

The *Hawgood* was winding its way up through the St. Clair River when they spotted a small package freighter at the dock, taking on its load in Sarnia, Ontario. "On a Sunday Morning" Kanaby recalls, "that's a long time ago. Coming through Port Huron, a fella says to me- see that ship? That's the *Regina*, a Canadian ship. I said looks like we're going to have company."

The *Regina* was loaded heavily with a general cargo for various ports around the lakes. It carried everything from champagne

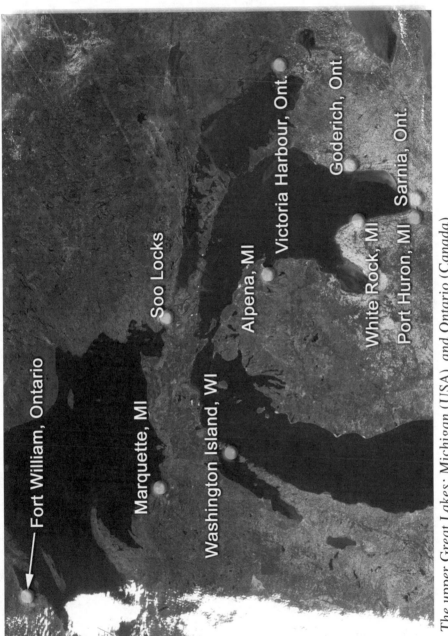

The upper Great Lakes: Michigan (USA) and Ontario (Canada)

Fort William, Ontario

Marquette, MI

Soo Locks

Washington Island, WI

Alpena, MI

Victoria Harbour, Ont.

Goderich, Ont.

White Rock, MI

Port Huron, MI

Sarnia, Ont.

3

Regina

bottles to barbed wire, and its deck was packed high with baled hay from the King Milling Company in Sarnia. Newspaper accounts say as many as eight train cars of canned goods were taken aboard, bearing labels destined to Winnipeg and 'points west.'

Kanaby steered past the *Regina* and sailed out onto Lake Huron. In a routine check of his pilothouse barometer, Captain Arthur C. May was undoubtedly surprised to see it nearly bottomed out.

The barometer is a simple instrument used to measure change in air pressure. This would be one of the earliest signs of a change in the weather, but this is usually indicated by a slight dip, hinting a low-pressure system was moving in. On November 7th, it was nearly bottoming out, showing a sharp change in pressure that would undoubtedly bring high winds. This was because cold air is heavier than warm air, and low pressure allows this cold air to rush in, causing wind.

Captains had to be excellent weather forecasters on the lakes, especially during the fall and early winter months. However few could have predicted what was happening in November of

4

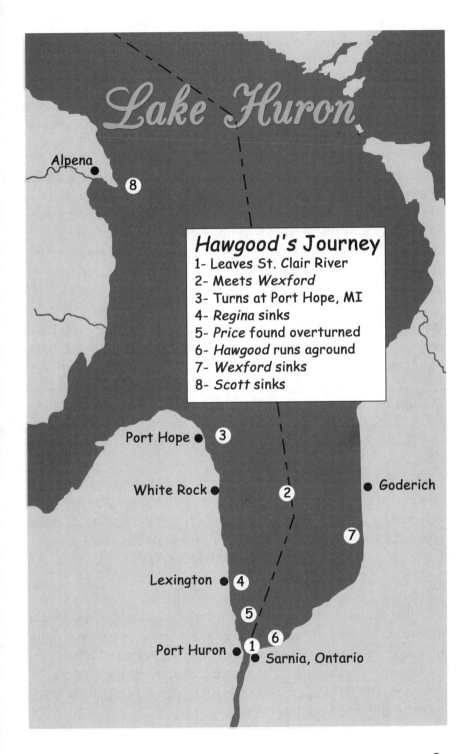

Hawgood's Journey
1- Leaves St. Clair River
2- Meets *Wexford*
3- Turns at Port Hope, MI
4- *Regina* sinks
5- *Price* found overturned
6- *Hawgood* runs aground
7- *Wexford* sinks
8- *Scott* sinks

Tracking the Hawgood's trip

1913. Weather historian William Deedler would later describe the phenomenon as a 'meteorological monster' in the brewing, feeding on moisture from the Atlantic Ocean and mixing with the Arctic cold descending from Canada.

Snow was one of the first signs of the storm for those without weather measuring equipment. A blizzard dumped three inches of powder throughout the Great Lakes as brisk winds pushed waves higher and higher. Around noon, Captain May knew it was time to seek shelter. There are few places to hide from a big storm on Michigan's east side, and he wasn't going to take any chances. Near Sand Beach, he ordered a turn to a southerly heading for the sixty-mile trip back to Port Huron. Just over an hour later, they again spotted the *Regina*.

If the *Hawgood* was considered a medium sized boat, the *Regina* was tiny. Her 270 foot length was critical for the ship's usual trade route, reaching through all the Great Lakes, down to Montreal and Quebec via the Welland Canal. Two hundred seventy feet was the maximum length for a ship that transited the locks at Welland, which lowered ships to the level of Lake Ontario and bypassing the impassible Niagara Falls.

Nearly half the size of the *Hawgood*, the *Regina* was having a tough time keeping course in the wind and waves. Kanaby believed he saw the ship's final moments. "On the way back, going south. I looked to the east and I didn't see that little boat anymore. It must have tipped over and sank. I think it was heading for Goderich, but never got there."

One lifeboat marked *Regina* came ashore with two frozen crewmen aboard. It was found beached across Lake Huron in Ontario, north of a little Canadian fishing village called Port Franks. Canned goods and other crewmen also washed ashore wearing lifebelts stenciled with the *Regina's* name, ending speculation that the long overdue ship had been lost in the gale.

If Kanaby and the captain's reports are correct, *Regina* would have been one of the earliest casualties on Lake Huron.

It is important to note that the only accounts from the *Hawgood's* travels are from Kanaby and a brief newspaper description of the voyage by the captain, written after the ship was stranded. Time had robbed Mr. Kanaby of many of the details of the storm, so it was difficult to get the exact route and time of when everything happened.

It is apparent that the *HB Hawgood* also turned again as it reached the bottom of Lake Huron, because Kanaby's narrative puts the ship much further north of where the captain reported he turned. This would certainly be plausible, as a similar steamer, the *J.H. Sheadle*, reported several tracks up and down Lake Huron. They could not see the shoreline, so they used 'soundings' to position themselves on the lake. This method employed a lead weight and rope, which was dangled over the side of the ship and measured after it hit bottom. These depths are compared to a map and a location is surmised from that. The captain of the *Sheadle* made a complete report of his travels after surviving the storm, as did several other captains at the bequest of investigators.

News accounts indicated the captain never took the *Hawgood* near the tip of Michigan's 'thumb', a narrow peninsula jetting out into Lake Huron. Kanaby reported that he saw the waves coming from Saginaw Bay, indicating that they made it near the mouth of this large basin before turning south for safety. This large basin's mouth is certainly subjective, as its boundaries are typically set from Point Lookout near Au Gres through to Point Au Barques. It could also be reasoned that the mouth is a straight line further north, starting at Au Sable Point through to Port Austin. Waves from that far north would have certainly affected the Hawgood's travels, and Kanaby's description paints an eerie scenario near what many historians believe to be the most dangerous place on the Great Lakes. "We went on north, and the seas out of Saginaw Bay looked like mountains," Kanaby recalled. "Oh, them seas was strong."

In the distance the wheelsman spotted a salt-water freighter. Its
shape was much different than the typical lake freighter, with its
pilothouse and engine 'amidships', or in the middle of the ship.
Ed did not recognize the steamer as it approached. "On the way
up, I looked to the east and there was another little boat. Don't
know what it was, but later someone said that was the *Wexford*."

The *Wexford* was heading south from ^{Wexford}Lake
Superior with grain for a small Canadian port city on Lake Huron
called Goderich. *Wexford's* crew was made up of sailors from
nearby Collingwood, and its captain was a well-known local
hockey star.

The last official sighting of the *Wexford* was by another ship
some thirty-five miles north of Goderich at 10:30am on Saturday.
Several residents of the town reported hearing her whistles at the
height of the gale. The steamer couldn't make it in to the harbor,
and instead sank with most of her upper decks wiped clean from
the ship by the storm. It's likely that the crew tried to escape the
ship as two engineers were recovered after the storm. Normally
the engineers remain at their stations during a gale, controlling the
throttles to keep the engine from racing. The second mate and a
few other sailors washed ashore close to a lifeboat found near St.
Joseph (just south of Goderich). What was left of the freighter was
found decades later in seventy feet of water about twenty miles
south/southwest of Goderich. You can read more about what was
found underwater at the end of this chapter.

Back aboard the *Hawgood*, the increasing northwest winds were actually helping the ship as it steamed south for Port Huron. Pushing the ship like a giant sail, the winds were also building the waves around the ship. On a course to hide from the storm, they were surprised to see a freighter heading out onto Lake Huron. Kanaby thought the crew was insane to take on such a gale. "I looked up ahead, here comes a boat. Oh that crazy man, coming out into a storm like this." Ed Kanaby described what could have only been a nightmare on the open lake. "About a 90 mile gale. How much stronger.. I don't know."

Charles S. Price

The undetermined ship was the *Charles S. Price*, loaded with soft coal in Ohio, heading north for a delivery to the far west end of Lake Superior. Kanaby wasn't the only person who thought the *Price's* captain was crazy for heading into the storm. The second engineer simply walked off the ship when it loaded in Ashtabula. Milton Smith had his fill of sailing the lakes and wished to spend more time with his growing family, and he would later tell newspapers that he had a premonition that the ship was in danger.

That is exactly where the crew found themselves, sailing into the storm near the bottom of Lake Huron. They would not make it much further, as a blinding snow storm called a 'white squall' obscured their path. These squalls can be so thick you can not even see the end of your own ship.

Kanaby described the worsening conditions off Michigan's thumb. "So, about White Rock.. it started to snow. And oh, how it snowed. What a blizzard. Couldn't see nothin'. So we kept on a goin' to see who it was. That was the *Charles S. Price*, loaded."

By 3:30 Sunday afternoon, the *Hawgood's* crew had lost sight of the *Price* and was pushing towards the southern shoreline. News accounts say the ship was about five miles north of the Fort Gratiot light when the crew saw another freighter. Kanaby remembers it was nearly a twin to the *Charles S. Price*. "We got by the *Isaac M. Scott* and the captain called down and said we're going to turn around and go in deeper waters. That scared me. I got scared."

Isaac M. Scott drawing by Capt. Bud Robinson

The *Scott*, bound for Milwaukee with a load of coal, would only make the northern reaches of Lake Huron. The waves were simply too much for the modern freighter and its rudder apparently snapped near Alpena, Michigan. Divers who later found the wreckage would note the rudder was ripped from the skeg, the mounting that let the rudder rotate to steer the ship. Without its rudder, the *Scott* would have fallen into a giant trough in the waves and rolled over. Like the *Regina* and *Price*, it would be flipped upside down... and no one lived to tell what actually happened. The damage to the rudder may also have occured when the ship hit the bottom of Lake Huron, smashing the fantail to pieces. One section still proclaims its name, albeit in segments. Kanaby still vividly recalled the building storm that would ravage Lake Huron Sunday evening. "The wind was strong and every few minutes a gust of wind come up, stronger than the one before. But it never ceased. It stayed right there until the next gust of wind would come up, still stronger than the one before." Captains would later report that the wind gusted to sixty miles per hour and raged steady for sixteen hours straight.

Kanaby had seen enough. He had a feeling that the *Regina* had been lost just after he saw it, and he knew others were in trouble as well. Captain May wanted to avoid the shoals and turn around and head north, keeping the *Hawgood* in deep water and away from running aground on the beach. He ordered the bow anchor dropped, which would use the wind to pivot the ship around back north. The anchor went down, but the wheelsman was not about to make the turn. "So he say's we're going to go into deeper waters," Kanaby remembers, " I said to myself, oh no you don't. Not as long as I'm a wheelsman. And I gave her a port wheel and threw the ship out of control, on purpose."

It is likely that the *Hawgood* was already out of control. By 9:30pm the winds were reaching their peak intensity and Captain May ordered a second anchor down, but it didn't hold. The lake level, which swelled six feet above normal, allowed the *Hawgood* to plow hard onto Weis Beach, near Sarnia, Ontario. When the storm calmed, the water receded and the ship's bow was high and dry in the sand.

Captain May never mentioned his wheelsman's actions in newspaper interviews. He told investigators that he was unable to see any lights or aids and he couldn't tell where he was until they came up on shore.

11

Hawgood on the beach

12

Kanaby believes in his heart that his actions saved the crew. "I think that's what saved the ship and the crew, by me throwing the ship out of control."

The beaching certainly saved their lives, as the storm's peak intensity was just a few hours later. Timepieces found on the lost crewmembers of the *Carruthers* and *McGean* (both ships were lost on Lake Huron) all stopped between 1:15am and 1:30, an indication that they fell into the water at that time.

Price turtled

The *Hawgood* spent these killer hours high and dry, although the waves did what they could to terrorize the stranded crew.

Kanaby wouldn't learn of the other ships he saw until that next day. A giant freighter was found floating upside down not far from where the *Hawgood* stranded. Spotted near the Fort Gratiot light, the 'turtled' hull made headlines all around the world. Newspapers guessed at the ship's identification for days until a hard-hat diver finally read it's name underwater. In the churned up lake water he felt the outline of the raised letters on the ship. Twice he spelled out CHARLES S. PRICE, just to make sure. News accounts reported that he searched the entire right side of the ship for collision damage, but found nothing.

That was not the end to the mystery surrounding this wreck. The body of the *Price's* chief engineer, John Groundwater, was found lying on the beach. Search crews found him near a *Regina* lifebelt and classified him as a deckhand on the tiny freighter. Milton Smith, the *Price's* second engineer who had left the ship before the storm, would correct the mistake. "That's him," Smith told the Thetford coroner. "That's big, good natured John. How the boys all liked him!" Smith also recognized the bodies of wheelsman Wilsie McInnis, fireman Chris Faulkner, and the ship's steward Herbert Jones, all who had washed ashore south of Goderich. "There he was," he told newspapers of his former cook, "lying there with his apron on and just as he looked hundreds of times when he was about to prepare a meal or just after he prepared it. Evidently the poor fellow did not even have time to look after his wife's welfare, which shows how quickly the boat must have gone down."

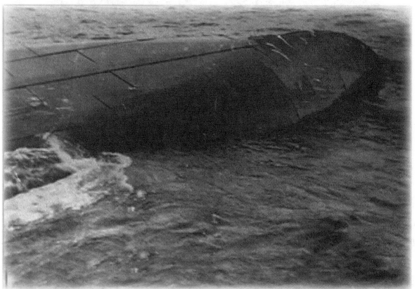

Port side *Price* bow

The assistant engineer concluded that the ship must have collided with the *Regina*. News reports were quick to report this as fact, and it was even romanticized to the point that some felt a rescue was launched from one of the stricken boats. Reports were also written on how the two crews were found wrapped in each other's arms. Surely this must be why the man had another boat's lifejacket on!

A better explanation would be found when authorities warned of prosecuting anyone who stole from the victim's bodies. An article in the Milwaukee Sentinel told of reports of looting near Port Frank when bodies were being robbed:

"The ghouls found the three bodies near the lifeboat of the wrecked *Regina*. The looters have made it more difficult for the authorities to identify the dead as the lifebelts have been taken away and the names on the lifeboats are missing..."

Ship captains were rumored to carry money belts with salaries inside, making for a tempting target lying on the beach. Other locals took souvenirs of the tragic storm. It is the author's belief that someone took the *Regina* belt from the beach and later tossed it near the body of the chief when police investigated. It certainly is not as heroic as a rescue attempt for the crew of the *Regina*, but it makes more sense. There are also no real details on how John Groundwater was found, or if the lifebelt was on him or near him. The reader must also note that the newspapers mixed up many details of the mystery, reporting it was a *Regina* crewman with a *Price* belt in some versions. The 'collision theory' was further debunked when the no evidence was found of a collision on the underwater hulks of the *Price* and the *Regina* some decades later.

Tugs pulled the stranded *Hawgood* off the beach several days later and damages were estimated at around twenty thousand dollars. It was a quick repair job, and Kanaby felt obligated to finish the season for Captain May. "We laid on the beach for a week, got pulled off and I made two more trips after that and laid her up in Buffalo." There's no doubt that Kanaby felt sympathy for his skipper, who would have been stranded again if his helmsman opted to stay ashore. "I was going to quit, but I was the only wheelsman on the ship so the Captain coaxed me to stay."

Captain Art May sailed the lakes for several more years and it is ironic to note that many of the ships he had sailed on were lost in accidents and storms. The *Merida*, which May skippered from 1901 until 1903, sank on Lake Erie in the Black Friday Storm of 1916. The *Mecosta*, which May commanded in 1899, was lost on Lake Erie in 1922.

Kanaby would spend at least another season on the lakes, sailing aboard the *B. Lyman Smith* and *CW Coxser*. By 1918, Uncle Sam came calling for help during World War I and Edward joined the Army as a flying medic. He returned home from France after the war to marry the sweetheart he met while training in Florida. They made their

home in Michigan, where Kanaby joined his brother Pete in elevator installations and repair. He would work on dozens of Otis Elevators in the tallest buildings in and around Detroit before going back to 'ground level';

Ed Kanaby photos courtesy Mary Jane Kasprus

returning to the farm fields of Michigan's thumb in 1937. Kanaby eventually owned two farms near Croswell, ironically only a few miles from the final resting place of the *Regina* and *Price*, the two

16

ships he last gazed upon during the King of Storms
Ed and Marcia's family grew to include five sons, three daughters
and dozens of grand children. He passed away on June 5th, 1993.

The *H.B. Hawgood* worked the lakes for another thirty years
after the storm. It was renamed *Pentecost Mitchell* and was
reconstructed in Conneaut, Ohio, in 1916. It finally succombed to
the cutting torches at Hamilton, Ontario, in 1946.

STORM FILE: 1913 STORIES

Size didn't seem to matter to
the 1913 'King of Storms'. It
would go down in history not
only for its winds and waves,
but because it swallowed the
most modern steel freighters
and tossed others ashore like
tiny toys in a giant freshwater
bathtub. Even Canada's largest
freighter, the 550 foot long
James Carruthers, was lost with
all hands somewhere on Lake
Huron. And while the list of lost

Louisiana burns 1913

and overdue ships continued to shrink during subsequent newspapers, it
was still a staggering
statistic- twelve ships
and all of their crew
were lost. Twenty-six
ships were pushed
ashore, many thought
to be a total loss.
Most were refloated
and repaired, with
only the *Louisiana*
as a total loss. It
caught fire after

Louisiana's Bow on the Beach 1993

running aground on Washington Island, at the tip of the Door Peninsula of
Wisconsin.

17

Plymouth after refit (Reid photo)

The barge *Halsted* found itself near the *Louisiana* when the gales picked up and they attempted to anchor inside Washington Harbor on November 8th. Battling blizzards and deep snow, the crews eventually made it to safety.

The real tragedy on Lake Michigan would be aboard a wooden schooner barge just north of Washington Island. Seven men sailing the barge *Plymouth* disappeared with their ship after being cut loose by the tug *James Martin*.

The story of this hapless barge is compelling and tragic, as we now know its crew was far from seasoned. Locked in a bitter legal battle with a local lumberyard, the *Plymouth* had former undersheriff Christ Keenan aboard as 'custodian'. The custody battle between the tug's owners and the CJ Huebel Company also landed the tug's regular skipper in jail. Captain Louis Setunsky was hired as master of the *Martin*, but the tug's owner and engineer, Captain Donald McKinnon, reportedly made most of the command decisions.

The *Martin* had pulled the barge away from the docks at Menominee, Michigan, on Thursday afternoon. Bound for Search

Bay (near Hessell, Michigan), their hopes to make the Straits of Mackinac were dashed when the winds picked up, so they instead anchored in the lee of St. Martin's Island for the evening.

After dinner aboard the barge, Marshall Keenan was given the choice of staying aboard the *Plymouth* or travel aboard the tug. "I wouldn't go aboard that old box. It is not safe," Keenan allegedly said, probably aware that the tug had recently undergone repairs to its rudder and planking in Wisconsin five months earlier. What Keenan didn't know was that the *Martin* was in worse shape than he thought. The *Plymouth* was in much better condition, having been rebuilt with steel arches after running aground

Martin and *Plymouth* loaded

in Marquette some 30 years earlier. In 1889, the shipyard at Bay City, Michigan, proclaimed the *Plymouth*'s new five-inch thick oak bottom made her a better craft 'than the day she was launched.'

The tug and barge combination made quite a team, and newspapers heralded their accomplishments, especially when they set harbor hauling records in July of 1912. The barge arrived in Menominee with 68,000 posts, no doubt putting a smile on the faces of the investors who had just purchased the barge. Aspiring for another successful season, the *Plymouth* was re-caulked for service in June of 1913.

Capt. McKinnon would later say he took this into account as the *Martin* sluggishly dragged the barge into the 1913 Storm. Located just north of St. Martin's Island, the tug was having a tough time pulling the giant barge through the waves. McKinnon would later write about the ordeal in a local newspaper. "I kept on 80 pounds of steam until 6 a.m. with two green firemen, one laying seasick in the forecastle, the other doing the best he knew how. At 6:30 a.m. Saturday morning Setunsky came back to me and said he was going to put the barge to anchor and I said I guessed that was the only thing left to do as he could not handle the tug. At that time the steam had gone down to 60 lbs., so I told him to give the signal to drop it. He did so and got no response from the barge."

With no answer from the *Plymouth*, the engineer shut off the engine and threw off the towline. McKinnon believed the schooner would be fine in the gale, telling reporters "she should have stayed there easy as there was a 3500 pound anchor, chain 1-5/8 inches thick, five shots overhauled on the main deck, 5 more in the hold, and the end shackled around tow posts and she was lying just about one mile under the lee of the Gulls. There was a schooner anchored at the northeast corner of Summer Island. They were getting three times the sea that the *Plymouth* was, and she was only one third her size."

The Door County Advocate described the storm as a 'regular old rip-snorter,' with the wind gusting so strong that the drawbridge was kept closed in fear that the gale would 'whirl the structure around.'

McKinnon's editorial wouldn't be the last word in the sad story of the *Plymouth*. The tug and its crew returned to Gull Island late Monday afternoon and found no trace of the ship or crew. The body of deputy U.S. Marshall Christ Keenan was later found 50 miles away in Manistee, Michigan. A note in a bottle, found near Mears, Michigan, told of the crew's toil in the killer seas:

"Dear Wife and Children: We were left up here in Lake Michigan by McKinnon, captain of the James H Martin tug at anchor. He went away and never said good-bye or anything to us. Lost one man last night. We have been out in the storm 40 hours. Good-bye dear ones, I might see you in heaven. Pray for me. Christ K. I felt so bad I had another man write for me. Huebel owes $35.00 so you can get it. Good-bye forever."

News accounts exclaimed that the only 'experienced sailor' aboard the barge was its captain, Axel Larsen. His body washed ashore weeks later near Muskegon. The body of a third crewman, 17 year-old Edward Johnson, was found at Platte Bay, Michigan. A week later, the tug *Martin* mysteriously sank at her dock in Menominee. Newspaper accounts believed it had been scuttled.

Local uproar led to an investigation that suspended the license of Captain Setunsky, because he wasn't qualified to skipper a tug of the *Martin's* size, nor was he qualified to sail to its destination of northern Lake Huron. Captain McKinnon's pilot's license was revoked for hiring Setunsky, and for not reporting the existing boiler problems to government inspectors. Both faced fines near one hundred dollars, but they were ultimately found 'not guilty' of abandoning the *Plymouth*.

Rudder on Washington Island

There has been a lot of speculation over the years to the location of the schooner-barge *Plymouth*. The author's initial research at Milwaukee's Public Library indicated that the *Plymouth*'s location was just off Poverty Island, found by some

Wisconsin wreck hunters. The location sounded suspiciously familiar. Skin Diver magazine had an article about Poverty Island dated far earlier than the supposed discovery date annotated on the library file. It told of the *Plymouth* in nearly the same location. The author contacted the diver who was interviewed for the article and learned no measurements were ever taken, no artifacts suggested they were from the *Plymouth*, and only speculation fueled its identification. This may have also led to the identification of a giant rudder on display at Washington Island. A small bronze plaque announced it was from the *Plymouth*, lost in a storm in 1913. Local legend said it was recovered near Poverty Island.

Logic prevents this wreck from being the *Plymouth* on many fronts. Why didn't lighthouse keeper James McCormick or any of the other lighthouse personnel report a schooner wreck so close to their duty station? How would it have sailed against 70 mile per hour winds over two miles from where it was left at anchor near tiny Gull Islands? Why didn't anyone report the steel arches that should have been found in the wreckage?

Keel and (below) engine parts of *Louisiana*

It would take ten years before a personal visit was possible on the remains of the wreck, which was within eyeshot of the lighthouse.

The isolation of this island stands out as one

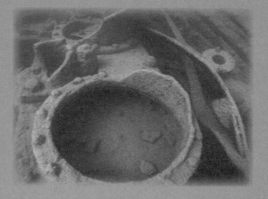

22

winds through the maze of reefs and islands in northern Lake Michigan.

We set out from Wisconsin, following around Washington Island to where the *Louisiana* lies. Burned to its keel, only pieces of the engine and some hull sections

Poverty Island Lighthouse

remain. The bow washed ashore many years ago, and what is left underwater is now covered with a thick coat of mussels. The author's first visit to this wreck was in the early 1990's, thankfully before the clams set in. Even then it was evident that the ship was salvaged, reportedly to take the boiler and engine out in 1920. What remains of the site was also extensively documented by student archeologists for the state of Wisconsin.

It's quite a long trip to Poverty Island no matter where you launch from. We traveled north of Washington Island to St. Martin's Island, and it was interesting to note that this is the site where the *Plymouth* and *Martin* had their final meal together. Once

Ron Bloomfield checks out Poverty Island's wreck

past the St Martin lighthouse, Poverty Island comes into view quickly. The author's dive team found the island was aptly named. We pulled near the shear rock face of the uninviting isle and raised the dive flag. I jumped into

23

Lake Michigan, ready to see a schooner lying beneath me. What I found was a jumbled mess of hulls that seem to crisscross in every direction. This wreckage does not have any steel arches, and it has obviously been extensively salvaged. It is certainly possible that the metal was recovered, but it is a better hypothesis that it is not the *Plymouth*.

The location fits better for the *Erastus Corning*. This two hundred foot schooner, once the 'Pride of the Lakes,' ran aground on the island in June of 1889. It was stripped by the lighthouse keeper within a month, and the ore cargo was to be salvaged as well. We did a short search grid out from the *Corning's* location to where the magazine map placed the *Plymouth* and found nothing.

It is the author's belief that the wreck is actually further south of Gull Island, where the water falls off to more than 100 feet. With little wreckage found from the ship, it is likely those huge anchors and chain are in this area, with the elusive *Plymouth* not far away. McKinnon told newspapers that most of the crew's belongings were aboard the larger Plymouth, so there is no doubt that incredible artifacts await exploration by the divers who locate this long lost barge.

---The 1913 Storm on Lake Superior

Lake Superior sailors did not escape the King of Storms. Not
only was the *Leafield* lost near what is now Thunder Bay, Ontario,
but several ships ran aground on Superior's southern shoreline.
Horrific winds during the early hours of Saturday, November
8th, slammed the steamer *Turret Chief* ashore on Michigan's
Keweenaw Peninsula. Seventeen lifesavers won gold medals after
rescuing twenty-two men and two women from the *L.C. Waldo*,
which had run onto Gull Rock near the tip of that same peninsula.
After a four-hour, thirty-two mile journey in a small lifeboat, they
chipped their way through thick ice to reach the stranded crew.
They survived
ninety hours
without food,
and a perilous
journey in
the small
boat back to
Houghton,
Michigan.

H.B. Smith

A lull in the
storm at Marquette, Michigan, convinced Captain Jimmy Owen
to leave the protected harbor around four in the afternoon that
Sunday. Newspaper accounts said other ships at port were amazed
when he pulled away from the dock without even sealing all his
hatches closed. The storm soon picked up and the *H.B. Smith* was
seen trying to turn around only to disappear into a blinding snow
storm. Wreckage from the ship washed ashore from Marquette to
Autrain; including a liferaft, mattresses, and a door. The body of
the second cook, Henry Askin, was found floating with a lifebelt

fifty miles west of Whitefish Point. An engineer was found a year later near Goulias Point, Canada.

Like the *Plymouth*, a message was found in a bottle, picked up by fishermen near Copper Mine Light in Ontario. Allegedly from the captain, it was dated November 12th, which led to some speculation of its authenticity. Eyewitnesses watched the ship leave November 9th, and it was unlikely that Captain Jimmy Owen would get the date wrong. The note claimed that the ship broke in two at Number five hatch about twelve miles east of Marquette, but as of this writing, the ship has not been found.

Wreck hunters are actively seeking the final resting place of the *H.B. Smith*, and the *Leafield* (lost near Thunder Bay, Ontario) in Lake Superior. The Navy was even coaxed into using some of the submarine-locating equipment for a peek beneath the surface off Marquette. Large boulders and iron ore deposits make the search difficult using traditional methods, and nothing substantial was made from the survey. Lake Huron also holds the secrets of the whereabouts of the *Hydrus*, as well as the largest of the ships lost in 1913, the *James Carruthers*.

Lightship 82- Before & after storm

----Lake Erie's Casualty

A message was also found from Lake Erie's only fatal shipwreck during the storm. *Lightship 82's* crew vanished when their ship was blown off station near Buffalo, New York. Scrawled on a piece of cabinet were the words *Good-bye Nellie, ship is breaking up fast. Williams.*

Captain Hugh William's wife Mary insisted that her husband never called her Nellie, and at least one local paper thought it was a hoax. Mrs. Williams herself went out in search of the lost lightship, but it wasn't found until that next spring, after extensive dragging of the bottom some two miles from the lightship's post. Only one of the six crewmen was found, washed ashore in Buffalo.

---Another Eyewitness

By 1993, only a handful of eyewitnesses to the storm were still alive to talk about it. The author was fortunate to find Ted Bullard right in his own backyard, living

Ted Bullard

in a retirement facility in Saginaw, Michigan. Mr. Bullard was eleven years old when a friend asked him to take a ride on his father's ship. Young Bullard and his friend Tom McCarthy sailed into one of the worst storms on record.

School would have normally been in session but a flu outbreak closed Goderich's classrooms for a few days. Tom and Ted headed north on a train to catch the steamer *Turret Cape* after it loaded grain. The equipment broke down, and Capt. Patrick McCarthy waited just long enough to take the boys aboard and head out onto Lake Superior. With winter freeze-up and a building storm on his

Turret Cape

mind, he wanted to get to the Soo Locks as soon as he could.

Superior raged as the *Turret Cape* headed south. It was so rough that they did not opt to turn around, and they slugged their way to the Soo. "The night before we left", Ted recalled in 1992, "the chef cooked a delicious chicken dinner. And the next day you could imagine what happened to the chicken dinner in those rough seas".

The *Turret Cape's* sloped sides looked more like a submarine than a traditional freighter, and it was constantly awash in green water during the storm. "Greenwater" breaks onto the deck and is deep enough to determine color. Spray is rarely given a second glance, but green water on deck means trouble. The design of the turret ship sheds this water quickly, instead of allowing its tremendous weight to do damage to the hatches.

When they made the Soo Locks, they had to continue on downriver. Ted remembers that the captain had few options. "There was no place left to dock, so we were forced out onto Lake

Huron, which turned out to be the roughest of all the Great Lakes during the storm."

Ted would later learn just how rough Lake Huron had become. The storm swamped the freighters *Argus*, *John McGean*, *Hydrus*, and three others before the *Turret Cape* would make it home. Just a few miles from the comforts of home, Ted learned he wouldn't be safe just yet. "When we got near Goderich there was no possibility of getting in there. The waves were 35-40 feet high, the worst they had ever been, and the wind was 90 miles per hour in spasms".

The Captain rode down the lake to Sarnia, Ontario, and spent the next two days riding out the storm. The crew managed to yell to someone on shore, and Mrs. McCarthy and Ted's parents were contacted and told that the kids and crew were safe. "They had no idea what happened to us and they were scared out of their wits," Ted explained. "When we pulled in, the town band was there, and most of the citizens were cheering and waving us in."

This wasn't Ted's first brush with death. Only a few years earlier he was canoeing in the same area outside of Goderich when the craft overturned. His friend drowned and Ted stayed with the upside down canoe. Rescuers found him underneath the boat, some two miles offshore. Only a few years later, he was steaming

Diver Bruce Campbell looks into the *Price*

past that location aboard the *Turret Cape*. "We were the luckiest people in the world; our ship design saved us."

Ric's Dive Log

EXPLORING THE 1913 WRECKS

I've often told lecture audiences about the strange connection I feel between the interviews I conduct and the ships that were involved in the tragedies. I have never been fascinated with the loss of life on the ships; that is simply the reality of what a shipwreck is. I'm more interested in the stories of the men and women who walked the decks and spent countless hours in the wheelhouse, engine-room or galley. Recently discovered shipwrecks offer divers a unique glimpse into a forgotten world. We all may have seen old photos or heard a song played in 1913, but would we recognize the technology or personal effects from this time period? Diving allows me to submerge myself into that moment of time, and if the waves and underwater currents are kind, I can see details from that exact moment when the ship met its end.

Price's anchor chain

Often my visit is well after the shipwreck was discovered, and sadly much of that evidence is long gone. Collectors have stripped wrecks of their brass and wheels, even bringing up planking to make tables and other curiosities. Long debates have ensued over the ethics of this practice, and I must agree that some wrecks are

30

SO wrecked that this is almost a flattering method of 'recycling.' But to take something from an intact shipwreck is a real transgression. These pieces will never grow back, and because technology has greatly changed our water transportation methods, we will never again see this type of equipment again.

A classic example is the *Charles S. Price*. It was known to millions after appearing as an upside-down shipwreck in countless newspapers. Dubbed the 'mystery ship', it baffled shipping experts until its name was finally revealed by a diver. Over the years divers have stripped the ship, taking oilcans, tools and other so-called 'trinkets'. They have also chiseled the name off of the *Price*.. so it is once again a mystery ship.

One of the first things you notice while diving the *Price* is that it is missing its rudder. I have not seen any record of salvage of this giant piece of metal, but an attempt to refloat the Price did occur in 1916. The rudder may have also broken off when the ship was floating upside down, the stern apparently scrapping bottom

Prop and Skeg of *Charles S. Price*

as its bow protruded up above the surface. The lost rudder could have also led to the ship's demise, as it is used to steer the ship and maintain a course through the waves. A broken or missing rudder would have certainly let the ship turn broadside into the winds, perhaps rolling over a ship that was already burdened with thick lake ice on its superstructure.

The *Price's* hull is rusted and slowly collapsing, so a journey inside is very risky. There is plenty to see from the outside, and its 500-foot length takes at least two dives just to see the entire hull. The giant propeller is chipped, perhaps from a river bottom or as part of the sinking. There is no telling how far the ship had drifted after it capsized, but rumors have always persisted about a giant pile of coal that isn't too far from the wreck. Where its cargo lies is where it turned turtle, an important clue to squelch the assumption that the *Regina* played a role in the loss of the *Price*.

Perhaps my favorite part of diving the shipwreck is approaching from the bow, gazing on the same view that was photographed when the ship was located after the 1913 Storm. The giant anchor chains are still in the chocks, dwarfing the diver as they swim in for a closer look. My hope is to return to the ship before it completely collapses from its own weight. It is interesting to note that I saw only a handful of zebra mussels on this ship when I saw it in 1993. Today the *Price* is entirely coated with clams!

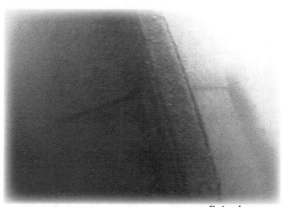

Price bow

Regina -

Substantial clues to the mysterious loss of the *Regina* finally surfaced when the wreck was located by shipwreck hunters in 1986. The boat was found upside down with its anchor deployed, and divers reported that the engine telegraph was indicating 'STOP'. It is very likely that the Captain called to abandon ship, and at least one lifeboat was released for a run to shore. Sadly, the closest shore was to the west, and the crew would have had to fight 60 mile per hour winds to get there. Instead they floated east at the mercy of the wind, crossing on a lifeboat to Canada. Not one sailor survived.

Regina's stern

Damage to the ship includes a large section torn open in its middle, but it is not characteristic of a collision. Both forward and aft deckhouses are buried in the sand bottom, but the name is still displayed on the stern.

Cargo from the *Regina's* holds would eventually make it to market. Salvaged after its discovery in 1986, bottles of scotch, spoons and other trinkets eventually found buyers in the form of souvenirs. *People* magazine featured a story on the recovery, stating that one bottle of 60-year old scotch sold for $8,000. Over 200 bottles of Champagne and 100 bottles of scotch were raised from the Regina, and a reported $100,000 salvage operation scoured the wreckage for a safe allegedly containing two million dollars in gold coins. That 'treasure' was never located and much of the upside-down interior of the ship was scoured in the search. What remains below today is protected in the Sanilac Shores Underwater Preserve.

Regina is one of my favorite places to explore, as the shifting sands cover and uncover artifacts every time I visit. Zebra mussels have greatly improved the visibility underwater, and it is possible to swim away from the wreck and see much of the stern. Upside down, you can get confused inside the wreckage. Many have explored into the engine room, but I limit myself to the incredible switchboard area and cargo hold, safely within site of a sun-lit exit. Beginning divers will be amazed just to swim along its giant prop and rudder!

Diver Greg Grieser on *Regina*'s prop

Wexford-

A Canadian fisherman located the sunken hulk of the *Wexford* in 2000. Last seen on course for Goderich, it was located 9 miles off St. Joseph, Ontario in 75 feet of water. Unlike many of the other freighters from the 1913 Storm, this ship is upright. This led to a quick identification, as the engine room and pilothouse were located amidships. Much of this superstructure is still in place,

Wexford- Capt. Bud Robinson

including a ladder leading to the missing pilothouse. A lifeboat davit also reaches up from the deck, complete with its pulley still in place. Tiny artifacts are found throughout the ship, but its grain cargo is long gone. Now divers can swim the length of its hull, illuminated by sunlight from its open hatches. This is a rare look at a shipwreck that has not been salvaged, and I really enjoyed my visit to this incredible underwater museum. Most people hope this new ethic of 'taking only pictures and leaving only bubbles' will protect this unique underwater museum from illegal souvenir hunters.

Anchor encrusted with zebra mussels

Diver Mike Peterson at *Wexford's* ladder

Diver Matt Crews at *Wexford's* lifeboat davit

Davit Close-up

Lloyd Belcher-
Wheelsman on the *Novadoc*

Chapter Two: "Safe Ashore"

Lloyd Belcher grew up in the small
lumbering community of Victoria
Harbor, located on the far eastern
corner of Georgian Bay in Ontario,
Canada. The son of a grain elevator
worker, he loved spending time with
his dad and brothers on the family skiff. With brothers Gordon
and Jack, he would spend his spare time splitting wood and doing
chores in addition to attending Mrs. Harrington's Sunday school
class at St. John's United Church.

Lloyd Belcher (family collection)

Lloyd's first job was at the local grain elevator with his dad,
earning a quarter an hour. When his dad died at age 57 from lung
complications, he knew it had to be from the dust at the elevator
and he looked to the harbor for another job. He saw others working
the boats making 30 dollars a month with free room and board,
and the decision to drop out of high school was simple. The village
was so small it only had high school classes for two years, and
only those with transportation could move on to graduate at nearby
Midland. "Well, in those days," Lloyd said, "that was 1936 and
there wasn't too many jobs, and to go to high school I'd have to
go to Midland, and it was quite costly.. so I said I'll go sailing and

see how I make out."

Belcher first sailed with Canadian Steamship Lines on the 416 foot *Prescott* until it was idled for lack of work. He joined the *James B. Foote* in the fall, working his way up from deckhand to watchman and eventually testing for wheelsman. In the spring of 1940, he shipped aboard Paterson's small canaller *Novadoc*. This freighter was one of 16 canal-size freighters built in England for the Paterson fleet. *Novadoc* was 260 feet long, just short enough to squeeze through the Welland lock system. This opened up markets from the upper Great Lakes into Lake Ontario and all the way to Montreal. The *Novadoc* frequented these northern Canadian ports, including trips up the Saugenay River.

Novadoc- Baillod Collection

Novadoc could carry a variety of cargoes, from pulpwood to powdered coke. Coke was used in the making of aluminum, and the freighter made several trips to Chicago to bring the material back to Montreal.

Belcher's venture into the Armistice Day Storm began with one such trip from Chicago, with a midnight call to take the wheel on his six-hour shift in the pilothouse. He recalls several other ships waiting to load in Chicago. "We were the first to load. There were two other Paterson fleet there. We got out about 5a.m. and as we went out the breakwater the captain yelled to the Coast Guard; they

38

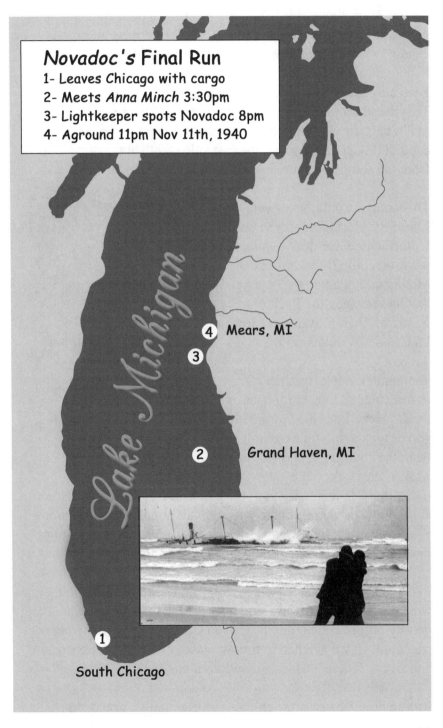

Novadoc's Final Run
1- Leaves Chicago with cargo
2- Meets *Anna Minch* 3:30pm
3- Lightkeeper spots Novadoc 8pm
4- Aground 11pm Nov 11th, 1940

Lake Michigan

④ Mears, MI
③

② Grand Haven, MI

①
South Chicago

had a station right there. We were right along side of them, and he asked for a latest weather report. They said there wasn't any change, so we figured we were going to be all right."

By 6 a.m., the windy city was starting to live up to its name. That didn't seem to worry the wheelsman. "When we came out of Chicago, it was blowing a bit but it wasn't too bad and so the captain thought he'd go up the east side and then the wind was from the southeast and we were protected on the shore."

This course would have been safe if the storm had stayed put. Unfortunately for the *Novadoc*, it was heading right for Lake Michigan. By noon, the "cyclone" that had ravaged the Pacific Northwest had moved from Iowa to La Crosse, Wisconsin.

Temperatures fell from the 60's to freezing, and the barometer on the *Novadoc* bottomed out. The waves took some time to form from the southwest, and Belcher walked the deck to the galley for a

Capt. Don Steip

cup of tea. He then headed to the pilothouse for his noon to 6pm shift. Few would be able to walk the decks later that afternoon. Wind velocities increased to 38 miles per hour, and a squall line developed right on top of the *Novadoc*.

"Through the course of the day the winds shifted around to the west; the south/southwest," Belcher recalled, "and the waves kept getting bigger and bigger. It was too late to go over to the other shore and so we just had to follow up, and it kept getting worse and worse. There was nothing we could do then."

Riding up the coast of Michigan, the decision was made to try to

40

return to Chicago. That meant a dangerous turn back to the south, and the crew was warned that the *Novadoc* would roll heavily. Around Muskegon, Capt. Donald Steip ordered hard-a-port, but the ship only made it half way around in its left turn. Lloyd said the ship just laid in the trough (the lowest part of the waves), and rolled. Huge breakers crashed over the stern and the ship was pushed north, headed for Little Sable Point.

High above the lakes, the storm's squall line was speeding towards Lake Superior, moving 350 miles in just six hours. Meteorologists calculated that the front raced at sixty miles per hour, passing Ludington between 1:30 p.m. and 2 p.m.. The winds soon

increased and a blizzard moved in by nightfall.

Belcher knew the *Novadoc* was really in trouble. By 6 p.m. his shift was over, but he stayed in the pilothouse to lend a hand. The high winds knocked out their radio antennae and tore at the cloth covers over the cargo holds. He wasn't thrilled about going out on deck in the storm, but knew that water in the hold would certainly mean that the ship would sink. "There was a split in the tarp of the number one hatch and the captain sent me out with another man and we found a board in the forepeak and we nailed it over top of the split in the canvas, and we made it pretty secure."

Soaked through, the men were sent to their rooms for dry clothes. It was then that the skipper tried a second time to turn the *Novadoc* around. The winds were at gale force now, and the ship wouldn't respond when the wheel was turned. Belcher remembers that it was tough to stand on the tossing ship. "It wasn't very good.. you had to hang on to something at that point. And then when we saw we were really in trouble he sent me down to tell the men to put their lifejackets on and come up to the wheelhouse." Belcher figured it would be too dangerous to go outside and climb down to the crews cabins. He went inside the Captain's stateroom and banged on the steel floor. Those below responded and Lloyd shouted to them through an open porthole. The off-duty crewmen grabbed their lifebelts and headed up to the pilothouse.

Fred Chessell (left) and Richard Simpell (far right)- Cross Collection

Glimpses of Little Sable Point Lighthouse were made as the tiny *Novadoc* crested the mountainous waves. The ship, pushed by gale force winds, headed uncontrollably for shore and was now buffeted by surf returning from the beach. Turning slightly, the crew felt they might be able to turn away from shore. The Captain ordered full power from the engine room in a valiant attempt to pull away. Now at the wheel, Lloyd remembers this final attempt at saving the ship. "At one point he put the chadburn at double speed, so the engineer would give it everything he had. I turned it hard a-port to try to straighten it out. Eventually we did get it out. We got it straight and a big wave came up and broke all the windows out, and then we were in water up to our knees then."

The flying glass hit nearly everyone in the pilothouse, especially the first mate, Richard Simpell. Lloyd said Simpell was cut pretty badly. "He was pretty close to the glass when it broke in the wheelhouse. It just missed me, I was lucky. He got the brunt of it and the water came right in with it.. it was quite a mess there for a little bit."

Firing a boiler- Friedhoff Collection

The crew in the pilothouse had a terrifying view of the building waves, but the men below decks never saw the fury of the storm. "It's terrifying, because you can't see what's going on," Howard Goldsmith said in an interview, "and the boat is turning every way but upside down. And you have no idea what it was like down in the fire hole. It was something else."

Goldsmith was a fireman aboard the *Novadoc*, and his challenge was to keep the boilers burning by shoveling in coal. "Firing the boat, there's something tricky about it. You take a shovel full of coal and when you go to throw it in you have to let the heel of the

shovel hit the deadplate. That way the coal spreads over the fire."
An "even" spread of coal meant it would burn more efficiently.
"You can't just throw it into a heap. That won't work. And that
was a hard thing to do with that boat rolling like that. You had to
wait until you were fairly level and then you could throw it in."

It was soon
apparent
that one man
couldn't fire
both boilers
in the tossing
ship. "You're
trying to keep
the steam up,
and it was a
hard job doing
it alone. So
Fred Chessel
(the 2nd

Howard Goldsmith in 2003

Engineer) knew what we were up against and he put four men
down in the fire hole to fire that boat, two men to each boiler. One
guy would hold the door open and the other would bail the coal
in."

The ship was slowly losing its battle with Lake Michigan, and it
passed so close to the Little Sable Point Lighthouse that lighthouse
keeper William Krull smelled the smoke from the *Novadoc's* stack.
Krull rushed into the tower and fired flares into the seventy-five
mile-per hour winds, hoping to warn the crew of the dangerous
sandbars off shore. He sighted the *Novadoc* a half-mile to the
south and heading for shore, watching the boat for thirty minutes
until it was just north of the light. Krull feared the worst as the
Novadoc's lights went dark, around 8:30pm. The lighthouse
keeper then attempted to call Muskegon's Coast Guard, but the
telephone lines were down.

The crew aboard the ship were well aware that they were going to run out of lake. "The second engineer said we're going aground." Goldsmith remembered, "He said I want all you people to go up into the oiler's room. That was on the lee side of the storm." The 'lee' is the side of the ship out of the wind, and the engine crew rushed to the small quarters on the starboard side of the freighter. It was there that he noticed two men were missing. "There were seven men standing in the oiler's room. Everybody from the after end, except for the two cooks, they were drowned."

Very few details exist regarding the loss of the two cooks, Joseph DeShaw and Philip Flavin. After the storm, a newspaper quoted *Novadoc* fireman James Quinn. "The bodies of (the cooks) were in a room off the main dining room. We made three or four attempts to get to them but we couldn't even get close."

Another news account reported the cooks were lost while trying to traverse the deck forward during the storm, but the only eyewitness I have found is Howard Goldsmith. He believes they were killed prior to running aground, and that they were not in the oiler's room with the remainder of the engine crew. "There was a skylight over the dining room and that skylight caved in, and when it caved in, it just washed them out. They went with it," Howard said solemnly, "You have no idea what that storm was like."

Another newspaper report simply read "Members of the crew who went to the rescue of DeShaw said he was killed almost instantly when a huge wave caved in the side of the cabin. Flavin was reportedly washed over the side soon after the damage occurred.

An Ontario newspaper talked to DeShaw's widow, who said this was his third shipwreck. The 63 year-old Toronto man had sailed since 1913, learning to cook in lumber camps.

The engine room crew were only in the oiler's room for a short time when the *Novadoc* shuddered and slammed into a sand bar just two miles north of the Little Point Sable light. Lloyd recalled that it didn't take long to get hung up permanently on the sandbar. "When we hit bottom, it just went bang. That's when the deck split and it filled up with water fast. When that happened, the captain told the mate to see if he could go down and drop the anchors, just in case that it started going back out again." The shattered windows in the pilothouse were allowing spray from the waves to hit the men and

STAR BRINGS WORD OF SAFETY TO SEAMEN'S PARENTS
With power lines out of commission as a result of the same gale which drove the freighter Novadoc aground in Lake Michigan, Mr. and Mrs. Matthew Goldsmith of Binghampton, Ont., did not hear the radio flash which told that their sons on the ship had been rescued. Told of their safety by The Star, Mr. Goldsmith embraced the reporter and cried: "Thank God—my prayers are answered." The two sailors are Clifford (LEFT) and Howard.

Lloyd said the captain had them go to his room for shelter. "The wheelhouse was so wet that we ended up in the captain's quarters and that's where we spent the rest of the time."

Belcher feared that there weren't many options for saving themselves. "We knew there weren't any lifeboats because they were broken up, and one went floating right past us. I was still in the wheelhouse when the starboard lifeboat let go. It went right up alongside us. But we thought it was no good anyways- we'd never get back there."

Goldsmith believed they never had a chance to get to the lifeboats. "Tons of water started dropping on us, and I mean tons of it. It just shook us to pieces, and don't think we weren't afraid. Because we didn't know at what minute everything would collapse around us."

The storm continued well into the night and the forward end

46

crew waited in darkness until morning. The boilers were long extinguished, so steam no longer heated the registers aboard ship. Belcher and the forward crew improvised a way to get warm in the ten degree temperatures. "We found a pail after daylight, a steel pail in the captain's room and we started breaking up furniture and putting pieces of wood in the pail and opened a porthole on the starboard side to let the smoke out and we took turns warming our hands. It gave us a little bit of heat- not a lot, but enough to warm our hands every once in a while."

It was much more uncomfortable in the oiler's room. Water poured in from all sides, and the men took turns bailing water out a single porthole. Goldsmith said no one really spoke during the ordeal. "You didn't want to talk, you just stood there and shivered. And I mean shivered."

In the captain's room the men passed the time with talk of rescue, and the first mate announced that he wanted to try and make it to shore by himself. "He [Richard Simpell] wanted to swim to shore with a line, but the captain wouldn't let him. There was no way he'd make it into shore. The water was cold with ice on deck, a lot

Onlookers helplessly watch the *Novadoc's* plight in the storm.

of ice on the winches, everything was coated with ice."

Richard Simpell was no newcomer to shipwrecks. Newspapers boasted he was in over 17 sinkings, most recently aboard the *Cartierdoc*. He was also on the *Huronton* when it collided with the *Cetus* in 1922. The captain of the *Cetus* kept the two ships together long enough to taken on the full crew of the *Huronton* before it sank in deep water in Lake Superior. Ten years later the *Huronton's* former skipper was aboard the *Novadoc* along with Dick Simpell when it hit the rocks near Alexandra Bay. A storm threatened to take the crew so they escaped in a lifeboat. The *Novadoc* was raised and refitted and believed to have sunk again during the summer of 1940. Historians argue over whether or not this accident occurred, but at least two sources claim that the *Novadoc* was laid up for repairs to its hull in July of 1940.

The Armistice Day Storm took the *Novadoc* to the bottom permanently. Photos and home movies show the ship on November 12th, with huge waves breaking over the superstructure. A small crowd had gathered on the beach, including Coast Guard personnel who were perplexed on how to get their rescue gear to the beach. Rescuers felt the ship was not in danger of breaking

Novadoc in the storm- Cross collection

Three Brothers II- Cross Collection

up and thought the members of her crew were safer aboard the shipwreck than by a rescue attempt during the storm.

Belcher and the rest of the crew of the *Novadoc* wholeheartedly disagreed. "We watched them, and to see all these people- we thought well, they're going to do something for us. I don't know what."

With no heat, food or safe drinking water, the crew was wondering if they would make it. By Tuesday night they had spent some 20 hours in the storm and nearly everyone in Pentwater heard about the stranded crew. Dozens of gawkers assembled on the beach, including a few automobiles. This made many people wonder why the Coast Guard could not find their way to the shipwreck. Clyde Cross was a local fisherman who knew he could make it. He went to the Coast Guard station and offered use of his covered fishing boat, the *Three Brothers II*. The government rescuers had little interest in his offer. Surfman Roland Ericksen told him to 'mind his own business.'

Soon night came to Pentwater, and the crew of the *Novadoc* were wondering if anyone would come to their aid. Forty-foot waves pounded relentlessly against the ship and Belcher said the ten men in the captain's room had to move when the storm finally crushed in the outer door. "During the night the winds went down a bit,

49

but the waves were
going up right over the
superstructure. The
outside door caved
in during the second
night, and of course
there was another door
between the captain's
quarters and where
the door broke open.
It was alright." The
crew moved into
the captain's office
and huddled in the
darkness.

Novadoc deck during salvage

Those on shore did
manage to send along
some encouragement
through the darkness.
"Every once in a while
at night they would flash their car lights and that meant something
to us," Belcher said. "And in the morning I took a sheet off the
captain's bed, ripped it in half and opened the door on the starboard
side and waved that sheet up and down."

The morning would get even better when the crew looked out over
the horizon, some thirty-six hours after running aground. "The best
thing that happened was after daylight, about 10 o'clock," Belcher
recalled. "We looked down and saw a boat coming out. That
was the three fishermen come out to get us. And I talked with the
fishermen afterwards and they said they were down at the beach
the night before, and they were pacing up and down and they said
next morning we're going to go out to get them regardless.. and
they did."

"We thought my God, someone is coming to our rescue!"

Goldsmith added, "And sure enough, that boat came up to the bow of the boat and took everyone off the bow and then came back to the stern of the boat. And the chief engineer and the second engineer stood there and helped us into the boat, and then they got in."

There is some confusion between the stories printed in the local papers and what the survivors told the author. One newspaper prints the heroic tale of the engine room crew's voyage along the broken deck to the pilothouse. It quotes Howard as the source who told them of the perilous trip along the frozen deck. *Howard Goldsmith of Singhampton, Ontario, another member of the crew, told how he and seven other shipmates crawled over ice-coated and storm-twisted steel bulkheads to reach the front of the vessel. "When the boat started to break up we crawled forward"* Goldsmith related, *"only an unbroken bulkhead made it possible for us to get there."*

Three Brothers II rescuing *Novadoc's* crew

Three Brothers II arrives with survivors at Pentwater

Eyewitness accounts of history are certainly our best source for exact minutiae of the account, but time frequently steals those precious details. The only trump to these interviews is actual film footage of the event. With the 1940 storm the author found that Burt Steven's home movies didn't add up to the legend of the gale. History has amplified the height of the waves during the rescue, and while it in no means reduces the accomplishment of the fishermen, it certainly was not as dramatic as published. The survivors described waiting for the boat to ride a swell to get parallel with the deck before jumping into the rescue boat. The footage doesn't show this and many times the author has wondered if the film was taken later during Clyde Cross's salvaging of the *Novadoc*. The home movies showed incredible footage of the storm and the actual landing

John Peterson is transferred to a stretcher

52

at Pentwater, edited in a way that made it look like the same day.

Lloyd Belcher (second from left) at the Coast Guard station potbelly stove.

Unfortunately, Mr. Stevens passed away before any details of his remarkable film could be clarified. It is the author's belief that it was all filmed on the same day.

Lloyd Belcher, who told me he couldn't remember if the crew came forward after the storm, did write about the incident in his account of the shipwreck shortly after being rescued: *"When daylight came the Captain went down to the after-end of the boat to see who was all there. We knew there was someone there as they were throwing water out a porthole. When they came back up forward we found to our sorrow that the cooks had been washed overboard and one fireman was almost all in from exposure. Seventeen of us were once more back together again and we all crowded around the fire. The fire felt good to them as they had no fire all the time they were there."*

The Coast Guard arrived five minutes after the rescue by the fishermen. Cross told the rescuers that all seventeen survivors were aboard his fish tug and the Coast Guard's open surf boat followed the tug back to Pentwater. Belcher could not believe all the people who had lined the channel to greet them. "It's a long breakwater going

L to R Joe Fountain, Corky Fischer, Clyde Cross

down and some of us rode on deck- others had to stay inside. The fish-boat had a long cover over it and so as we went along we could see people on the docks watching and taking pictures and we landed at the Coast Guard station and that's where we got off and went in."

John Peterson was the only survivor that went directly to the hospital. He would remain hospitalized for over a year, due to severe injuries to his legs. Peterson wrote two letters to Captain Cross, mentioning electroshock treatments as part of his therapy.

Howard Goldsmith described what happened once they landed on shore. "They took us out and into the station. And in the Coast Guard station was a big pot-belly stove, and it was warm. And they brought out all the rum we could drink. I had three or four

54

shots of rum. I dearly loved rum." Lunch was served to the sailors, and it was still vivid in Goldsmith's memory. "I never saw a pile of sausages like it. That platter must have been three feet long and the sausages were two feet high."

The local telegraph company allowed the crew to send messages home for free. Belcher's message was simple, "SAFE ASHORE. HOME SOON." It brought incredible relief to a family that had heard their son was lost. "My dad was deer hunting two hundred miles north of Victoria Harbour, that's where we lived, and they had a battery radio. The first report was that we were all gone. And then after he got home, they said there might be life. Then they got another report that some were drowned and some were saved. Then when they got my telegram and they knew I was alright."

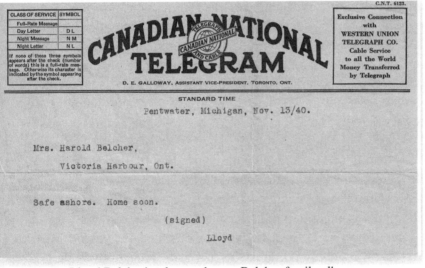

Lloyd Belcher's telegram home- Belcher family album

Captain Steip tried to show his gratitude to Cross and his fellow rescuers Joe Fountain and Gustave "Corky" Fischer. Steip reached into his pocket and pulled out a wad of cash- some later saying it was well over a thousand dollars. Newspapers noted that Cross refused it, but subsequent accounts say his partner took it and promised to split it three ways. It was later reported that Cross invested in a brand new tug to replace the 'oldest fish tug in

Pentwater' with a new 40' tug built by Edvard Pederson. The *"Clydie C"* was launched during a maritime festival in Pentwater, christened by Clyde's daughter Barbara.

Clyde Cross and his new tug- photos courtesy Barbara Cross

Newspaper headlines transformed Cross into a daredevil superhero, but not everyone was cheering. The Coast Guard chief at Grand Haven criticized the fisherman for a 'lack of cooperation.' Chief Boatswain's Mate Alfred M. Anderson later testified, "When we were endeavoring to launch our surfboat in Pentwater Lake about 8 a.m., it became stuck in the mud. I called to Cross's tug, which passed within 100 feet of us on its way out, to help us. But they ignored our call."

Cross maintained that he had engine troubles on the way out and left Joe on the wheel while he and Corky poured water on a frozen pump. No one was blamed officially, but there was certainly enough doubt regarding the so-called 'snub' that the trio were rejected as Carnegie Award winners. This medal, awarded since 1904, is awarded to civilians who risk their lives to save others. The author contacted the Carnegie group regarding the rescue, but the official response was that they were confident in the investigation of facts from 1940 and had no intention of re-opening the nomination.

The 'civilian' rescue had many in the Coast Guard wondering what happened. Doug McCormick, a Coast Guardsman who took on that same storm in a tiny boat to help another shipwrecked crew on the far northern shore of Lake Michigan said, "I couldn't understand that. I figured it was a Coast Guard job. There shouldn't be anything too rough for a surf boat. I never refused to go out."

News editorials also chided the Coast Guard cutter *Escanaba*, the local rescue ship which missed the storm because it was laid up in Manitowoc "to get some new gadget installed." The editorial went on to explain, "The *Escanaba* has been in Manitowoc since October 6th. If she can manage to stay until spring, her white paint won't be scratched or her table silver marred by such uncomfortable events as November gales or the rigors of winter navigation."

The criticism may have been on target for the Armistice Day Storm, but not for the *Escanaba's* overall record. It had several rescues to its credit and by Coast Guard estimates had saved over six-million dollars in ships and their cargo since it was launched in 1932. Tragedy would befall this cutter when it mysteriously exploded and sank while on convoy duty in June of 1943. This remarkable history is told in the next chapter.

Cross in his tug

Ultimately, it was the chief of Grand Haven who would be 'reprimanded' for the fiasco on Juniper Beach. Alfred Anderson, who first responded to the beach but did not get his lifesaving equipment near the *Novadoc*, was held up for promotion to full boatswain. Officials told newspapermen that the storm, which also pushed the car ferry *City of Flint* aground at Ludington, depleted Coast Guard resources and that Anderson lacked the experience to know his job thoroughly. The report said there was a passable road that could have been used by lifesavers, "but it was not discovered

City of Flint aground near Ludington

by such personnel." A letter published in the newspaper reflected how many in the community felt about the fishermen, who all received bronze medals from the local VFW. Joe Van Arendonk of Pentwater wrote "You may not wear a uniform with stripes neatly pressed, with brass buttons polished. You may not always have a clean shave with shoes nicely shined. But you are deliverers; you are lifesavers."

Novadoc after the storm- Cross Collection

The Canadian government showed their gratitude by issuing a silver Sheffield platter to Captain Cross. Joe Fountain and Corky Fischer both received letters and checks for twenty-five dollars. It is interesting to note that a single lawyer involved in the 'official investigation' of the sinking of the *Novadoc* was paid well over a thousand dollars for his efforts. Reams of paperwork are in the Canadian archive regarding the process of requesting the platter, which would later be donated by the Cross family to the maritime museum in Pentwater, Michigan.

Salvaging the *Novadoc* with the *Three Brothers II*

The storm's fury would finally be tallied to include two more freighters; the *Anna C. Minch* and the *William Davock*, and two fish tugs and eight fishermen. The devastation to local fishnets would cause several businesses to go under. Charlevoix alone would have over forty-thousand dollars in damaged equipment, and it was hoped insurance relief would help the industry get back on its feet. The commercial fishing industry on Lake Michigan was already on its last legs. A botulism scare in the 1960's nearly shut down commercial fishing; trout numbers were decimated by the sea lamprey, and perch and whitefish numbers decreased.

Clyde Cross left the lakes for ocean fishing in 1949, searching for tuna off Southern California. The last commercial fish-tug left Pentwater after the spring of 1970.

"Corky" Fischer, who had bought his own fish-tug in 1941, met up with Lloyd Belcher when the former wheelsman camped in Pentwater in 1983. Fischer died at age 79 on June 15th, 1989. Clyde Cross passed away in California after a bout with pneumonia on April 15th, 2002. The author is gratefully in debt to his daughter Barbara for sharing her family scrapbook with me. It had articles sent to Clyde from most of the *Novadoc* crew, and also had personal letters of thanks and Christmas cards that add a personal depth to the rescued crew.

One of the greatest mysteries is the whereabouts of Joseph L. Fountain. The last newspaper interview from Corky Fischer said that Fountain went to the Detroit area and was not heard of again. Very few details can be gleaned from what information can be found on the rescue, except that he was Native American and some called him "Injun Joe." Social security records and death certificates have not revealed any clues as to what happened to him. When the Canadian government tracked down the 'official' spellings of the names for the cash awards and silver platter, they said he was Joseph L. Fountain. It is important to note that this 'official' document had Corky's last name incorrect; as Fisher instead of Fischer. So it is anyone's guess from the plethora of newspaper attempts like Fountain, Fontaine, Fontane and others.

Joe Fountain recovers lamps

Howard Goldsmith, who was shipwrecked with his brother Clifford on the *Novadoc*, never returned to the lakes. "They knew that I never wanted to go sailing again. I really didn't want to go sailing in the first place. I could make more money cutting wood than sailing. But, my brother, he wanted me to go and I wish that I hadn't." Goldsmith became a maintenance welder for General Motors and married a schoolteacher. He was surprised when the author called asking for a television interview. "What amazes me is that it happened sixty years ago. And why did they wait until now to bring up the story? Why didn't they do it twenty-five years ago, when all the main characters were alive. They have to wait until Lloyd and I are almost dead and it's something I can't remember."

Lloyd Belcher made it his mission to remember. He wrote an account of the ordeal for a presentation at his church and later spoke twice at the library in Pentwater. Belcher personally knew many of the sailors that died aboard the *Anna C. Minch*, which was sunk just a mile north of where the *Novadoc* stranded. He had last seen the freighter making its way near Grand Haven. *Minch's* lifeboats and grain cargo

Lloyd and his new car

washed ashore along with seven bodies. Belcher's girlfriend lost her brothers Clifford and Howard Contois to the storm. He took Helen and her mother to Toronto to identify their lost loved ones. "When we got to the morgue I opened the car door and opened the door for them and they wouldn't go in.. they said it was too much. They couldn't go in. So I went in and identified them."

In an interesting twist to the story, it was Clyde Cross who first discovered the whereabouts of the *Anna C. Minch.* He was checking his nets for damage when he spotted what looked like a seagull on the waves. It turned out to be the jackstaff of the ship, barely breaking above the waves. He could make out the green painted hull of the *Minch,* just below the surface. Divers would later discover that this was only the front section of the ship. It took several months before the after-end was located, nearly an eighth of a mile away. The storm had

Minch pennant

erased the superstructure from both sections, leaving only the deck and open hatches. A giant gash in the ship led many to speculate that the ship had collided with the *Davock,* but that steamer wouldn't be located for another thirty years. Inside the *Minch's* engine room, divers would find the last two of the nine recovered sailors.

While it is unknown if radio would have helped the *Minch's* crew

Anna C. Minch- Baillod Collection

during their ordeal, it is sad to note the ship was to get a ship-to-shore phone in late November. Stranded so close to shore near the Pentwater Coast Guard station, it may have brought help to a crew that most definitely could see the shore as the storm ripped their ship apart.

The *Novadoc's* wheelsman gave up on the lakes for a while, driving cargo in a truck. This land route would prove nearly as dangerous, as he was a passenger in a car that hit a Grey Hound bus head on. Belcher was asleep at the time of the collision, which killed his employer, Mobe Denure and friend, Bill Stewart. Just as sad was the fact that a hitchhiking soldier was also killed in their car. The collision evidently happened in a blinding snowstorm on the way back from dropping off a truck for overhaul.

Belcher returned to the lakes and sailed with Algoma Steel for a while, later joining the Canadian Navy as a quartermaster aboard the frigate *Matane*. History would again affect his ship while he was at the helm, this time during World War II off the coast of France.

On July 20th, 1944, the *Matane* was hit by a Nazi glider bomb. "The Germans had a bomb they could drop from a plane way up in the sky and radio it down. We turned one way and it turned too." Belcher was amazed at

Lloyd Belcher, HMCS

how the bomb chased them down. "We couldn't get away from it.. it hit us not too far from the wheelhouse, about 15 feet from the wheelhouse."

The *Matane* was seriously damaged and seven men were killed. Most of the remaining crew left the ship, but Belcher stayed aboard until it was put into a floating dry-dock near Scotland. By the time he was reassigned, the war was over. "The day I discharged, they asked me if I wanted my old job back. I said no.. I was

HMCS Matane

finished sailing forever. So I went building houses for Conn Smythe, he was a builder and had at the hockey team here." The former wheelsman learned carpentry through a six-month course through the Department of Veteran Affairs, but soon grew weary of working outside during Canadian winters. He took a job with A & P stores as a finishing carpenter, responsible for installing shelves, counters and office equipment.

A blind date with a nurse from Leaside found true love, and Lloyd Belcher married Barbara in 1957. They had three sons; two work in heating and cooling, and a third managed a grocery chain. Lloyd stayed with A & P for 38 years. Nearly all the stores in Ontario, Quebec and Manitoba show his craftsmanship.

One of the author's fondest memories was with Belcher and his wife Barbara when they traveled with him to visit with Howard Goldsmith in 2003.

Lloyd and Barbara Belcher, 1957

64

The author had no idea the former wheelsman was recovering from knee surgery when he asked the duo to take a stroll on the beach. Belcher never complained as he waded through the muck at Wasaga Beach to film scenes for the documentary "Safe Ashore."

Lloyd Belcher passed away three years later at the age of 86. He

Barbara Belcher, Howard Goldsmith & Lloyd Belcher, 2003

had planned his funeral long in advance and asked that "Will your anchor hold" be sung at his memorial. Written nearly 60 years before the Armistice Day Storm, it was eerily similar to the wheelsman's close-call on Lake

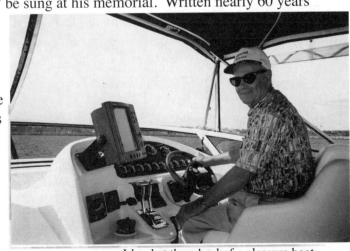
Lloyd at the wheel of a pleasure boat

Michigan: "Through the tempest rave and wild winds blow, not an angry wave shall our bark o'erflow. We shall anchor fast by the heav'nly shore, with the storms all past forevermore."

The *Novadoc* became quite the tourist attraction after its stranding. Even the author's grandparents traveled from Muskegon to see it.

Clyde Cross was asked by Paterson Shipping to take anything of value from the ship. Photos in Clyde's scrapbook show the *Three Brothers* tied alongside the freighter, with Joe Fountain offloading lights and other gear. Locals eventually took everything else of value.

The Coast Guard, who were beaten to the wreck by the fishermen, finally did get a rescue from the *Novadoc*. Jerome Jorrison and a friend became stranded on the shipwreck when their boat drifted away during a photo excursion.

Spray-painted warnings were put on the side of the ship, telling people to stay off the wreck. That winter, ice coated the vessel and the crushing bergs and waves eventually took their toll.

The tall smokestack and superstructure fell into the lake and most of the superstructure was ripped from the hull. The submerged wreck was marked with a buoy for many years. Today the buoy is gone, but wreckage rises dangerously near to the surface on the

stern. Mostly buried, you can still make out much of the bow and some of the space below decks. Only a quarter of the ship is visible, and each year different sections reveal themselves to those who explore. It can be snorkled, but it is a tough swim from the beach.

STORM FILE: 1940 STORIES

Historians still argue over what storm was the worst on the Great Lakes. It depends upon your criteria for 'worst'; whether that be the most lives lost, most damage, most ships lost or highest sustained winds. The 'King of Storms' is aptly named, as this series of gales took a dozen ships and sent them to the bottom. Two hundred forty-four lives were snatched in one violent weekend, and the damage was near 4 million dollars by 1913 standards.

It was also unique in that it sank ships on four of five Great Lakes, with only Ontario missing the tragedy of the storms. But for highest recorded winds, the 1913 Storm couldn't touch the 1940 Armistice Day Storm.

This storm made headlines when it was 2,300 miles away from Lake Michigan. On November 7th, forty-two mph winds oscillated in such a way that the brand-new Tacoma Narrows Bridge was literally shaken apart. Once the third longest suspension bridge in the world, the bridge plunged into Puget Sound below. Cars were stopped on the bridge during the accident, but only a small dog lost its life in the disaster. The remains of the bridge now lie in 180 feet of water.

Bridge Aftermath- WSDOT

The storm raced across the United States, and by late November 10th, the Weather Bureau placed its center over Kansas City, Missouri. Storm warnings were hoisted at 6:30 a.m. that next day, when the storm raced into central Iowa and developed into a severe storm. Winds were brisk at eighteen miles per hour on the lakes with moderate rain reported on Lake Michigan.

The Weather Bureau out of Chicago would record it as "one of the most severe storms ever recorded in that section of the country," and that November would go down as the snowiest November ever on record. And while the forecasts did indicate bad weather, no one was prepared for what happened on Lake Michigan that night.

Earlier on November 11th, the skipper of the steamship *Saturn* was questioning the forecast he heard earlier that morning. He tapped his falling barometer and it kicked back slightly. Captain Ralph Fenton would state "...instead of holding steady or indicating a northeast storm, she kicked back. That made me suspicious of the weather report, so from then on instead of going back to get breakfast at 6 o'clock I went right up in the pilot house and told the Third Mate to contact KDA at Chicago and find out the weather across from Madison."

At 7 a.m., the 420 foot bulk carrier *William B Davock* was making

William Davock- Baillod Collection

its way towards Chicago. Loaded with coal at Erie, Pennsylvania, Captain Bill Allen had already endured a rough trip on Lake Erie. "It's 80 miles from Buffalo to Erie and we rolled all the way, beam wind and strong seas. The third mate was seasick, besides other members of the crew," he wrote to his family. "Don't know how many more trips we have, but hope this is all."

Capt. Billy Allen- courtesy of his family

The *Davock* crew had been into Chicago twice before, and the skipper told his family he spent the last trip trying to keep them from "killing each other." Capt. Allen wrote, "Three firemen and 3 oilers all got drunk in Chicago last trip and took some along with them, alcho rub(sic) and etc. And one went crazy and one got DT. We couldn't get any men and took them to Buffalo.. all but one, he got off in Escanaba."

The *Davock* was followed down the lake by the steamer *Henry Steinbrenner*, which was also headed for South Chicago with a load of coal from Ohio. The *Steinbrenner* passed the *Davock* at 2 p.m. near White Shoals and the two chased each other towards Illinois, ending up near Ludington at 7 a.m., November 11th.

This was the time scheduled for a routine check with Interlake, and Captain Allen had the advantage of using a wireless telephone to call the front office at 7 a.m.. Reporting in twelve miles east of Ludington, Michigan, he stated all was well with the ship and crew. The ship then called radio station WMI in Lorain for a position report.

In his letter to his family, the captain had hoped to make south Chicago by midnight, but increasing winds were slowing his ten-knot progress. His radio traffic indicated the ship would make Iroquois by 1 a.m. and that the weather was from the ESE with haze and light rain.

It was around this time that they were passed by the steamer *Crowley*, which was traveling northbound for Lake Erie. Captain Albert Hayden remembered radioing the *Davock's* mate Leroy Shirkey that the storm was building. "I discussed with the 3rd Mate the probability of *Davock* coming [from the north] and mentioned that his respit would be of short duration on the east shore as the strongest winds would come from the westward at that time we were about seven miles below Little Sable."

Capt. Fenton aboard the *Saturn* began criss-crossing Lake Michigan, attempting to find the least amount of waves. He believed, like many captains, that the next wind would be from

the northwest, so he hauled over to the west shore. Mother
Nature worked her best to fool him, switching from SE to SW and
catching him as he neared St. Martin's Island. He took no chances
and hid behind the island until the next morning.

Myron C. Taylor- Great Lakes Lore Museum

Several skippers would witness the lowest barometer reading of
their careers at 2 p.m., when the squall line ripped through. A
one-hundred mile per hour wind hit the *Myron C Taylor* at 2:15
p.m., and the barometer dropped to 27.80. The wind stove in his
observation room windows, despite the steel shutters that were
in place to protect the quarter-inch glass. Captain Henry Leisk
reported that the *Taylor* was outrunning flying birds. "It was
blowing so hard that we were going faster than wild geese, they
couldn't go into the wind." It was the worst that Leisk had ever
seen, even when he survived the 1929 storm that sank the car ferry
Milwaukee.

In Detroit, the 78 mile per hour winds were swaying TV and Radio
broadcast antennas so badly that people called police. WJR's 733
foot radio tower, reportedly the highest structure in Michigan,
toppled to the ground, causing over 60 thousand dollars in damage.

The 'world's largest electric sign' also was wrecked in Chicago.

The gale damaged several freighters, slamming in their dining room doors and flooding rooms. The lighthouse at Lansing Shoals reported a gust at 126 mph that blew in their portholes. Cocooned by a thick ice coat, the men inside were powerless to the storm, and Captain William MacBeth aboard the *George Perkins* reported the tower looked like an iceberg. The *Perkins* later lost an anchor and 80 fathoms of chain when the winds snapped his shackle. The skipper also said his radio direction finder was lost to the winds, reducing his ability to discern his location. He would later find shelter with four other freighters under Garden Island in upper Lake Michigan.

The *Henry Steinbrenner's* captain caught one final glimpse of the *William Davock* as they attempted to ride out the increasing winds. "Eighty to one hundred miles an hour.. it was a twister." Captain Laurence Jones would later tell investigators. He believed the *Davock* was 'making from Grand Haven,' and he attempted to update Captain Allen with the weather report from Port Washington. Within twenty minutes the conditions had changed, with a wind shift and pouring rain. "I tried to call the *Davock* twice to give the report from Port Washington but I couldn't raise him on the telephone. After the gale hit us, I didn't try to contact him any more."

At four that afternoon the waves were battering the *Henry Steinbrenner*. The skipper reported damage to his lifeboat from a rogue wave and a cross sea that was causing heavy rolling. The hurricane force wind only lasted for twenty minutes, but raged on at 60 to 75 miles per hour until 4 a.m.. At 9:30 Chief Engineer Paul Olsen reported the two studs were pulled out of the eccentric strap and he told the captain that he was shutting down the engine. Now in the teeth of an all night storm, it was hardly the time for a breakdown. The winds took the ship and pushed it into a trough. Within fifteen minutes the repairs were made and the engine was restarted, but it took twenty-five minutes with the wheel hard over to correct her course. Ice buildup on the decks coated their lifeboats with an impenetrable jacket, making it impossible to even think of launching. In the engine room, the chief and mates took turns 'throttling' the engines, cutting power when the waves raised the prop out of the water. This prevented the engine from racing without the strain of resistance from the water. They continued riding the throttle until eight the next morning.

The *New Haven Socony* had its pilothouse blown away, and the skipper navigated from the upper deck using a flashlight and compass. A huge sea hit the ship, disabling control of the ship from the pilothouse. The captain went aft and shouted orders down to a crewman on the emergency wheel. The *J.C. Allen* was radioing for help near Grand Haven, reporting to station WAD that her steering cable had snapped. The *Peterson* had the same trouble at the top of the lake, drifting in the gale with a broken rudder until it plowed onto St. Helena Island. The skipper thought he was 50 miles south near Fox Island. The *Pathfinder* finally grounded near Escanaba and the *Sinaloa's* skipper, Captain William Fontaine, began to wonder if Death's Door was the place to be during a storm. They had sheltered near Washington Island after taking on 5,500 tons of sand from Green Island. Now the sand sucker was dragging anchor and Captain Fontaine needed a better place to hide.

Doug McCormick was a Coast Guardsman stationed at Plum Island, near where the *Sinaloa* was waiting out the storm. The men talked to the ship via radio and told them the barometer was quite low and that they expected a shift in the wind. Captain Fontaine took his

Doug McCormick

chances out on the open lake, hoping the change in wind direction would work in his favor. McCormick says they clocked a gust 105 miles an hour at Plum Island and soon heard that a ship was in trouble. "We got a call that the steamer *Empire State* had lost her steering. They called a guy from Milwaukee and they wanted to know if we would pick him up." McCormick and the Plum Island crew took their motorized thirty-six foot lifeboat and headed to Ephraim, Wisconsin. They picked up the ship's electrician, but

were unable to approach the *Empire State* with the seas at thirty feet. They returned the electrician to shore and were soon called to go after the *Sinaloa*. Around Monday at midnight the anchor had finally snapped off and the radio went dead. Five hours later the boilers went dead and the ship

Sinaloa aground -courtesy Superior View Studio

was at the mercy of the winds. It rammed into shore near Fayette, Michigan and then dragged back out to Sac Bay, finally running aground near Burnt Bluff. Locals witnessed the *Sinaloa* on the rocks and Captain Fontaine sent a note in a bottle to shore so the locals could tell his owners what happened. Officials were notified and the Plum Island crew set out into the storm to help.

McCormick remembered Lake Michigan's storm changed, now being ravaged from the southwest, pushing the surf boat towards Michigan. "I was steering, I remember Marcus Olson- he was in charge and then we had Phil Peterson aboard and he said Marcus you'd better steer, but he said ole Mac is doing fine! I'd go up the peak and it would twirl right around! And did we make time going up to Burnt Bluff. As the temperature went down to 14 below zero we were icing up pretty bad and we had about a foot of freeboard."

Meanwhile, local fishermen at Fairport were assembling their own rescue team. The after crew, who had been huddled in the galley, tied a rope to a buoy and floated it ashore. It was tied to a tree and fishermen Tom Peterson and Cecil Shawl used it to get their 16 foot rowboats out to the stranded ship. Shawl told his grandson in a recorded interview,"One of em' had a wooden leg. He had a little trouble sliding down the rope, they had to slide down a rope into our boat, and when we started back I told the men to hold on."

Capt. Tom Peterson (right) Courtesy Benjaman Peterson

Tom Peterson's boat capsized on the way back to shore. "The other boat flipped right over with all the men on it, right in the water. I'll say one thing, the State Police were there and they weren't afraid to wade out in the water and help them guys." By 5 p.m. the first 13 were removed. It took four more hours before nine more would make it ashore from the galley of the ship.

McCormick and the Plum Island crew arrived just as the Marquette crew was setting up their breeches buoy (newspaper accounts say it was the Munising crew). They watched from their lifeboat as the forward crew were removed. It's fair to say the rope was strained when Captain Fontaine hooked himself into the breeches. McCormick knew the skipper was going to get wet. "He was about four-hundred pounds, maybe five-hundred. He was underwater most of the time." The second mate, Harmon Burch, was the last of the forty-one men off. They warmed themselves at a giant beach fire and then were taken to Garden and Escanaba.

The Plum Island crew were happy to see the waves had diminished for their ride back to Washington Island. They were surprised to find the *Empire State* inside the harbor, her flukes broken by the waves, but in relatively good shape. Just to the east side of the lake the steamer *Conneaut* had run hard aground on Lansing Shoal. It lost its rudder and prop and was pulled off only a few days later.

In all, some fifty people were killed on the lake; dozens more died while hunting in Minnesota and over a million turkeys were reportedly killed by the Armistice Day Storm at farms from Wisconsin to Illinois.

Novadoc bow and deck winch

Minch stern bollards and bass

-Diving the *Minch, Davock* and *Novadoc*

The *Novadoc* still has much of its shape, but the *Minch* looks nothing like a ship. Locals tell me the wreck was blown up by the Army Corps of Engineers as a navigation hazard, and I certainly believe it. Forty feet deep, these wrecks are often damaged by ice, but not to the point where you can't tell stem from stern. Only the presence of anchor chains offer a hint that I'm on the bow, and part of the hawse-pipe sticking up indicates that much of the hull is now gone. This wreck is often swarming with smallmouth bass, and machinery and the occasional ladder remind me that this was a place where people worked rather than a fish habitat.

Minch's anchor chain

Those anchors do help me envision what the final moments of the ship might have been like. The chains are buried deep in the sand, and it's possible the captain of the *Minch* ordered

Diver on the *Minch's* winch- courtesy Rod's Reef

those hooks dropped to prevent going ashore. Divers who visited the ship in the fifties mentioned the wreck was on rocks, but today sand envelopes the wreck.

The stern section still contains the giant boilers, and the doors

Coal in *Minch's* firebox- Rod's Reef

are open to reveal pieces of unburned coal. Video shot before the zebra mussel invasion shows much more detail. Today much of the engine is buried, and I hope one day these sands will move out to reveal more detail to the wreck. And while I haven't been able to make out too much from what is now left of the ship, the divers' observations from 1940 do paint an ominous last few moments of the *Anna C. Minch.*

Clyde Cross noted only the forward section of the *Minch* was found, 400 feet from shore with 120 feet of the stern missing. Coast Guard telegrams indicate that some of the deckhouses, wiped clear of the hull, were spotted nearby. Once the steel pilothouse and other superstructure was lost, the crew had no protection from the storm. The temperature plummeted and the men succumbed to exposure from the elements.

A ladder pokes out of a hatch on the *Minch*

Diver Leo Mahan said there was a twenty-three foot gash in the port side of the ship, near the number-one hatch. He reported the hole started at the bilge and ran clear up to the spar deck. The metal was bent inward, as if another ship had hit it. Many marine experts felt this could be from a collision with the *Davock*, but the testimony of Mahan showed similar damage to the opposite side as well. Nearly the whole side was collapsed, mostly on a forty-five degree angle. His measurement was 230 feet from stem to the tear and he reported four hatch combings intact without their covers.

Engineers measured the bow section at 150 by 50 feet, lying in a northwest-southeast direction with only six feet of water over its end. Five hundred feet away they found the missing stern section, about 200 feet long. Both sections faced the same direction, towards shore. Four months later, Leo Mahan dove the stern section. Deep within the ship he found two more bodies. One was under the throttle, and he believed it to be the engineer. He said the throttle was open and the engine was in full reverse. The second crewman was reported to be in a nearby companionway. This is the best evidence that the ship was still under power when it came to shore. A clock was also found in the engine room, its hands frozen at 11:48. Investigators didn't pay much heed to the timepiece, which was given to the insurance company. If the clock was working, it would have indicated the *Minch* did weather the storm for some time before finally succumbing to the waves. It is known that the ship tried to ride with the waves, turning around when it realized it would never make port in Chicago. This is evidenced by the fact that the *Novadoc* saw the *Minch* around 3 p.m. by Grand Haven, and the ship was wrecked some fifty miles further north.

The tug owner who was assisting during the October survey testified in the investigations that he heard the diver found both steering wheels lying in the engine room, still attached to their cables. The room that housed these wheels was missing. This is likely the emergency wheel of the *Minch*, and it certainly indicated the ship lost its ability to steer. A.E. Bonner also stated that the diver found three buckets, presumably referring to propeller blades. Two were chained together, a third was jammed beneath the tiller. This was the steering mechanism for the ship, and if the diver was correct, it would have crippled the ships ability to maneuver in the storm. The rudder was found turned hard over, and Bonner guessed it was hard a-port. It's not hard to imagine this heavy equipment smashing around on deck during the height of the storm, wedging into the tiller and preventing the ship from steering into the wind. In the trough of 40 foot waves, the *Minch* would have taken the brunt force of one hundred mile per hour winds and had its steel deckhouses sheared right off. The thought that a loose prop blade could cause damage has also come to light recently. Some have theorized that 'runaway' buckets may have caused the topside damage to the *Edmund Fitzgerald*, causing it to take on so much water that it listed dangerously low during a 1975 storm. Stored on deck in the middle of the ship, the *Fitz* could have lost a vent and a fence rail to the propeller blade, allowing for a boarding sea to push her nose down for a deadly plunge into Lake Superior. Whether that prop blade was a factor in the *Minch* disaster will never be known. I explored the emergency tiller when I dove the wreck, but the quadrant and machinery that controlled the rudder are either missing or deeply buried in the sand.

Minch's tiller pokes above the sand and debris

Both lifeboats from the *Minch* were recovered, but mariners know they could never be launched successfully in a hurricane. Heavily damaged during their trip ashore, it's not likely they would have been much use. It's interesting to note that of the major storms I have researched, no one survived in a lifeboat. The pontoon rafts, which work no matter which way they flip, have saved lives when the *Bradley* and *Morrell* were lost.

Today the wreckage of the *Minch* is only a fraction of what divers saw in 1941. Much is buried in the sand, and other material was either salvaged or blown up. Many of the winches remain, which leads me to believe there wasn't much of a salvage attempt. Located just a few feet below the surface, it was a navigation hazard to other ships. I'm sure it was loaded with dynamite and flattened out on the bottom. The

Sheila Frid on *Minch*- courtesy family

most striking artifact I saw was a huge mooring bit, surrounded by three smallmouth bass. It was on this bit that the Chief Engineer's daughter perched on for a photo just before the sinking. One of the most poignant repercussions from having these shows on PBS is that I get calls from all over the Midwest after my documentaries air. This has connected me with many who lost loved ones to the storms. Sheila Frid was kind enough to share memories and photos of the father she barely got to know. Chief Vincent Reive's body was never recovered.

Diver John Steele found the upside down *William Davock* in 1972. Located nearly 10 miles from the *Minch*, it's not likely the two collided. In over 200 feet of water, it's difficult for a thorough survey of the *Davock*. We did run sonar over the area, picking up a large coal pile and some structure behind the wreck. It's my hope to visit with a robotic camera and check the entire wreck for clues. Captain Allen's family hopes this will be the case, asking me to share everything I can about the storm and what might have happened. The most telltale info would

Sidescan image of *William Davock's* upside down hull

(Left) Cable stays apparently used to hold the stack in place. Depth 203'- Jeff Moore

be inside, located in the stern. My guess is that the ship lost rudder control, like so many others did in the Armistice Day storm. You may recall that this was likely the demise of many of the steel freighters lost in the 1913 storm as well. At least three of the ships had damage to their rudders!

We sent a diver down to the wreckage but found our mooring was off the wreck, snagged on what looked like the smokestack. Jeff Moore explored the site but was limited to only 20 minutes or so at that depth. The entire fantail, including the name and reported broken rudder, were not visited. Because of the depth, my hope is to return with an underwater Remote-Operated-Vehicle and explore the site at length. This would allow for detailed observation of the bow where any evidence of collision would likely be.

The most famous of the 1940 wrecks is the *Novadoc*. It seems that everyone in Pentwater Michigan knows about this wreck, and I should have asked a local to help us find the remains BEFORE setting out to dive it. The buoy that marked the wreck for decades had been removed only a few years prior, but the

Author swims above the smokestack

Novadoc is still a popular snorkling spot. The waves cover and uncover the wreck each season, and we were lucky to record the wreck when its bow section was fairly exposed. Sand buries over

70 percent of the *Novadoc*, and with limited visibility underwater you need to approximate the direction to swim to get to the stern. The fantail rises dangerously close to the surface, but our first visit left no  clue as to how much of the steam engine had been salvaged over the years. A return to the site in 2008 proved that the engine top was visible in the sand and that part of the boiler is now uncovered. Giant winches can be seen from the surface, less than six feet to the deck. It's a popular place for fish to hang out, but I'd be careful motoring over the wreck with the shallow clearance!

Some of the *Novadoc's* lower decks can be explored, but the sand prevented any real look inside. A diver can swim to the portholes in the fantail, and I wondered if Howard Goldsmith ever peered out those windows during his short career aboard the freighter.

Only time will tell if more of the *Novadoc* will be uncovered, but I'll continue to follow the progress of this ship. Now that the final survivors of the 1940 storm have passed on, I feel a special obligation to keep an eye on their ship.

Ray O'Malley,

Helmsman on the *Escanaba:*
Chapter Three: Honor Guard
for a Lost Crew

Ray O'Malley

Raymond F. O'Malley was born
on May 4th, 1920, and spent most
of his life in Chicago, Illinois. He
was quite comfortable in the water,
learning to swim at the local "Y"
by age 10, and even becoming a
lifeguard so he could swim in the
pool for free. Many summers were
spent on Lake Michigan, jumping into the sparkling green water
from the pier at Belmont Harbor.

With such a love for the water, it was no surprise where O'Malley
went for enlistment into the service. Joining the Coast Guard, he
would be surrounded by water; he just didn't know that it would be
mostly ice.

Right out of boot camp he was assigned to the cutter *Hamilton*
(WPG-34), training as a seaman apprentice to learn the ropes.
He was soon placed in the engine room, training as a fireman.
O'Malley advanced in rank and was transferred to the *Frederick
Lee*. O'Malley considered that new billet lucky because he would
have been in the engine room when the *Hamilton* was torpedoed by
Nazi sub U-132. Twenty-six men were killed. The *Hamilton* was
taken under tow, but it rolled over and was later sunk as a derelict,
becoming the first Coast Guard loss of World War II.

Much of O'Malley's patrols would be in the mid-Atlantic between the Azores and Bermuda. "Now, at the beginning of my service, we weren't in the war yet, and we didn't have radar. We were on what they called at that time 'weather patrol'. It was supposed to be a thirty day weather patrol, but you were gone for maybe sixty days at a time because you waited until the other ship would come on station. You had to wait until it got there."

America may have not been in the war, but the threat of Nazi submarines was all too real. The threat of German attack didn't scare O'Malley. "Someone a long time ago said to me 'were you ever scared?' I had a tremendous scare. I was in the crows nest on lookout watch and the ship.. that mast.. came down to the water, and I didn't know if we were going to come back the other way. And that's the only time when I really had a scare- where your adrenalin really goes. It was in the crows nest I got my first and last scare."

O'Malley and his crew returned to Boston where he would spend a few days in mid-March on leave before heading back to the North Atlantic. In a strange twist of fate, his ship would leave without him, and he transferred as helmsman to a 165-foot cutter called *Escanaba*.

The *Escanaba* left the naval drydock on March 17th, returning to Argentia Naval Base in northern Canada. The cutter was assigned to convoy duty, protecting ships as they crossed to and from Greenland. On June 6th, the "*Esky*" joined what would be its final convoy.

Escanaba was assigned as part of Task Unit 24.8.2 to escort convoy G.S. 24 from Narsarssuak, Greenland to Newfoundland. The cutter teamed up with several other Coast Guard vessels to guard the transport *Fairfax* and tug *Raritan* to St. John's.

Boatswain's Mate 3rd class O'Malley was new to the *Esky*, but was quite experienced in convoy duty. He saw much of the early days of the war aboard the cutter *Spencer*. "Many times we ran into

86

Cutter *Escanaba*- Ralph Roberts Collection

what was called the wolf pack and especially at night you would see two or three freighters would blow up. While I was aboard the *Spencer* we had two definite submarine sinkings or kills as they were called."

The movement of convoys was certainly considered secret. For several months the Americans had been building a series of airbases on Greenland, designed to not only help ferry aircraft from the states to Europe, but also to help move cryolite. This mineral was vital to the production of aluminum, and was found in abundance on the frozen continent.

But Nazi spies did know quite a bit about the airstrips and the movement of troopships. They even broadcast their knowledge, taunting those who listened to radio programs from Berlin. William Joyce had such a program, playing British and American music to entice the Allies to listen. He taunted the British over the airwaves, and was dubbed 'Lord Haw Haw' because of his regularly scheduled tirades against those who opposed fascism. But it was hard for servicemen not to take him seriously, as much of his inside information was right on the mark.

Ray remembers listening to the radio just before the convoy left Greenland. "He came out approximately June 10th or 11th and he mentioned the *Fairfax*, an AKA (transport ship) that hauled personnel. They were taking on civilians that had just built an airport at Greenland at BLUIE West One. He came out and said the *Fairfax* would never reach the United States. They knew all about it and they knew it was leaving and where it was at."

William Joyce after capture

Early reports of U-Boat sightings didn't help increase morale as the *Fairfax* prepared for departure. Two cutters were dispatched to take a look at Brede fjord, but they found nothing. They rejoined the convoy on June 12th, running through icebergs and dense fog as they departed Greenland.

O'Malley says the crew never spoke about what might be 'out there'. "I never heard anyone say 'God.. we're going out here, and we're vulnerable to the wolf pack.' None of the men ever said that. You would get up and go to the mess and there were more discussions on the food than the situation you were in. You were always in danger."

The convoy moved northwest to pass around the ice field to a position some ninety miles off Ivigtuk, Greenland. It was now Ray O'Malley's turn at the wheel. "At ten minutes to five they came back & woke me up to go on watch on the helm. I got out of my bunk, went up to the helm and relieved the man at the helm. I had time for one zig and that was the end of the zag."

O'Malley later told investigators that he heard something that sounded like machine gun fire, possibly the noise a torpedo makes while tracking. The static apparently caused the deck crew to investigate the port side of the ship, and the resulting explosion sent Ray upward, hitting the overhead. Ray described the aftermath in the official report on the sinking:"The Junior O.D. told me to step up out on the wing of the bridge. I noticed his face was all cut and bleeding. As I started for the door I picked up my lifejacket, put that on. I reached for the doorknob on the starboard door and there wasn't any, and in pushing against it, it fell right out."

In an instant, the *Escanaba* was gone. At 5:10am the crew aboard the nearby cutter *Storis* reported seeing a 'large sheet of flame and smoke' off their port bow. Two miles away from the *Escanaba,* they estimated it sank in just three minutes.

O'Malley watched the cutter fold up upon itself, breaking into two pieces. He sank with the ship, but was blown upward when another explosion occurred. He believes this was the depth-charges on deck, set to explode at a certain depth. The next thing he remembers is swimming to a large pole in the water called a strongback. This was a telephone pole sized piece of wood with cloth bumpers wrapped around it, used to keep the lifeboats from banging into the ship. Those lifeboats were dragged to the bottom of the ocean, some two miles deep.

O'Malley's official statement says it was an ensign that made his way to the strongback with him. It was a fifty yard swim to the floating log. "There was a guy next to me in a lifejacket and he said 'help me' so I grabbed the collar of his lifejacket and swam to the strong-back. I pulled the jacket up on the strong-back and there was no one in it. He froze- passed out, I guess. As soon as you pass out, you're down. So, that was my big hero thing.. that didn't work. I had an empty jacket and I dropped it."

Mel Baldwin was an *Escanaba* crewman who had just gone off watch at midnight and was sleeping in his bunk two decks down when he was knocked out of bed by the explosion. He told investigators that many of the crew from the starboard side of the ship were now on the port side."The ladders were pretty badly torn up, but I was lucky enough to get out, and I got up to the next deck and several of the men up there were lying around on the decks, I guess they were dead. I started up the next ladder and was told that other fellows had started up that way before and could not make it. I was half way up that way anyhow so I thought I would keep on trying. I was lucky enough to make out on deck. When I got there I noticed that the life boats were both gone, and the life rafts were torn up and the ship all the way aft was just in splinters."

Time has stolen many of the details of that morning from O'Malley. " Now, looking around I see at least four or five men. I'm swimming to this strongback and the captain is with me. I forget who else. I don't remember Baldwin, but he was on the strongback when they pulled us out of the water. Both of us were unconscious."

Escanaba's crew next to strongback (pole on right) USCG Photo

O'Malley's near-death experience was far from what he had thought it would be. "People talk about... ya know... when they die they see their life go before them.. I saw nothing. I just froze." What will never fade is the horror of the ocean's cold grip on his body. "Water temperature was like thirty degrees. You can only live in that water three to four minutes and that's it."

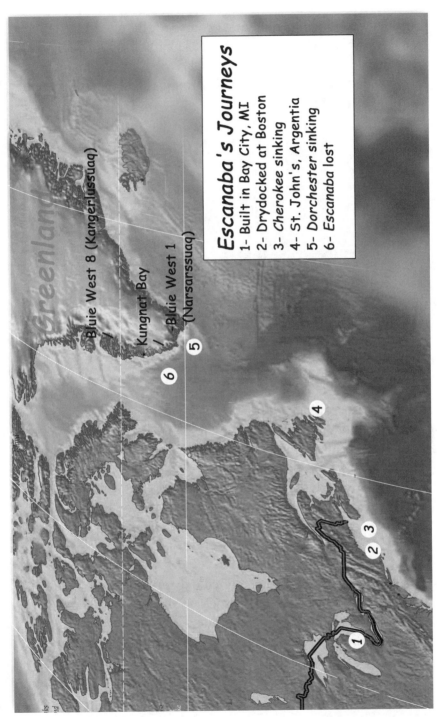

Greenland

Bluie West 8 (Kangerlussuaq)

Kungnat Bay

Bluie West 1
(Narsarssuaq)

Escanaba's Journeys
1- Built in Bay City, MI
2- Drydocked at Boston
3- *Cherokee* sinking
4- St. John's, Argentia
5- *Dorchester* sinking
6- *Escanaba* lost

The cutter *Storis* immediately set course for the site of the sinking, some two miles off their port bow. The harbor tug *Raritan* was also signaled to go in and look for survivors. The *Raritan* was commanded by Captain Sidney K. Broussard, who knew some of the officers on the *Escanaba*.

Tug *Raritan*- Courtesy Canonie Research Library

Captain Broussard recalled the sinking in a recorded recollection forty years later. "The general alarm bell went off in the cabin where I was sleeping and somebody came to the head of the ladder and hollered down, something like, 'come on Captain, the *Escanaba* is gone.'"

Broussard immediately went to the bridge to see what was happening. "I took a look where the *Escanaba* ought to be and there was nothing over there but oh like a cloud of water vapor or steam or smoke or something."

The first ships on the scene reported only an oil slick, bits of cork, several empty life jackets and one six foot section of what appeared to be a mast. *Storis* went to screening duty, looking for a possible submarine. The *Raritan* slowed to investigate further. Its captain watched for signals from the other ships while searching the area. Broussard remembers finding only small traces of the lost cutter, "quite a bit of debris in the water, a lot of paper, papers, you

92

know; documents or something."

No radio messages are sent during an attack, so ships use a system of flags to tell each other what they are doing. The captain noticed the *Storis* had the black pennant hoisted. "The black pennant meant that I have underwater sound contact with a submarine, stand clear of my sonar range, the range of my sound gear. So, I obeyed what the pennant said." The cutter then used its signal light to tell the *Raritan* to go in and pick up survivors.

Broussard recalled that no large pieces of the 165 foot long cutter were found in the debris. "I went on in and through all the litter, I looked over to port and there was a strong back, it is a spar, wooden spar, that holds the boat out. And hanging on to this thing appeared to be two men covered with oil, no lifejackets, just barely hanging on. To the starboard, over to the right was an officer in full uniform, khakis, cotton khakis with his shoulder boards, the whole thing, he had everything but his medals on. And he still had his cap on, lifejacket, floating good."

The *Raritan* skipper recognized the officer as Robert Prause, the second in command on *Escanaba*, and he pulled the *Raritan* right alongside the spar and stopped the ship. Broussard says Bob Prause was waving at him, and the dilemma was to choose who would come aboard first. "I don't care what you are doing, you help the guy that needs help the most. And that is exactly what I did. The boys threw a couple of heaving lines over and the one guy appeared to be unconscious. They were so traumatized by the cold and the explosion itself, that they couldn't reach over and get a line."

The *Raritan's* crew would have to jump into the icy waters to help O'Malley, Baldwin and Prause. Captain Broussard witnessed the extreme cold of the water as the rescuers jumped in. "They no more than hit the water and started trying to work on these people when the shock of the cold hit them and just about knocked them out. And I've seen people freeze to death in water like that more

93

than once. It doesn't take long."

The three survivors were aboard in five minutes, but it was no easy task. Broussard recalled that the water was black with fuel. "The *Escanaba* was an oil burner and that bunker oil is very thick, especially when the water is that cold and slippery. It is just a bloody mess. But they heaved and pulled and yanked and they kind of come up like in a bunch, in a bundle or something onto the deck."

Mel Baldwin- Courtesy Beverly Baldwin

Taken below to the crew's mess room, the young sailors came around quickly. They put Lt. Prause on a mess table and Broussard remembers they started artificial respiration. "You put the fellow on his stomach and try to get the water out of him the best you can and then press down, lift, press down, lift and some of the other people move the arms and legs and that sort of thing. On Mr. Prause it didn't work."

The crew tried to revive the Lieutenant for forty-five minutes, but realized he was gone. The captain told his men to put his deceased friend in an adjoining bunk in his quarters. By now the ocean was raging in a storm, and waves were breaking over the tug's bow. Broussard remembered how it affected the crew. "It was rougher than hell, you know, the further you got away from land and my crew was incapacitated by the rough seas. They were seasick, except for the chief engineer. I stayed on the wheel for seventy-two hours. Part of the time I'd stand and sometimes I'd sit on a

Mel Baldwin (l) and Ray O'Malley (r) on *Raritan-*

stool to try to stay awake. There came a time I went down to the cabin, I forget who took the helm, but somebody must have, and I was going to rest a little bit."

Ray O'Malley knows who took the helm. By then he realized how sick the crew was, and he offered his skills as a coxswain. "I don't know what day I woke up.. but I got up out of my bunk and Baldwin and I are up on the bridge, and the only one up there is the Lieutenant. He's handling the ship, and he looked at us and said, "Boy can I use some help."

Captain Broussard retired to his cabin, only to find his deceased friend. "I looked over there at Bob Prause's feet and I said, well that doesn't hardly make sense."

The skipper told his men to prepare the lieutenant for burial at sea, wrapping him up and looking for something to weigh the body down with. The chief engineer had previously scrounged some radiators from a wrecked ship in a fjord, hoping to use them in a new home stateside. Broussard ordered the chief to deep-six his heaviest artifact. "We didn't carry a lot of stuff on that thing, except Gardner's radiators and things. I didn't want to use a box of ammunition, we might need it on the way home. So, they lashed the radiator to Mr. Prause's feet."

The skipper knew something had to be said on behalf of the lost

Captain and officers of the *Escanaba*- USCG Photo

officer. "I said Bob Prause was a fine man, a good officer and a good sailor, and may God rest his soul. And then we put him in the water. The water was clear as glass and I will never forget looking down there and seeing my good friend, Bob Prause, sinking down with that radiator tied there. I ran up to the wheelhouse and that was that."

The tug arrived at the Argentia Naval base and the two survivors received orders to fly to Boston and eventually go home for 30 days leave.

PE-73

NAVY
~~TREASURY~~ DEPARTMENT

UNITED STATES COAST GUARD

c/o Postmaster, New York, N.Y.

U.S.C.G. RARITAN.

18 June, 1943.

From: Commanding Officer.
To: BALDWIN, Melvin A. (225-296) B.M.2c.

Subject: Temporary duty; upon receipt of these orders.

Reference: Verbal orders C.T.F. 24

    1.   Upon receipt of these orders you will proceed with O'MALLEY, Raymond F. (203-867) Sea.1c. to the STORIS for quarters pending air transportation to the Unites States.

    2.   As senior man you will be responsible for the execution of this order.

H.C. Brush

E.C. BRUSH.
By direction.

Original orders to leave *Raritan*

Back home, the war had strained the U.S. economy. Fund drives were set up to raise money for the war in every county, and people were saving scrap metal, nylons and rubber to help in the war effort.

Over thirty billion dollars had been raised by two earlier War Bond

97

drives, and President Roosevelt announced a third bond drive on the eve of Italy's surrender to the Allies: "Every dollar that you invest in the Third War Loan is your personal message of defiance to our common enemies, to the ruthless savages of Germany and Japan. And it is your personal message of faith and good cheer to our allies and to all the men at the front."

This bond drive would require constant reminders to the American people about the war, and in many cases it was desperately needed. Truancy and accidents at industrial sites were slowing supplies from reaching the troops, and the military needed a way to get workers back on track. Having two survivors from a cold-blooded submarine attack would be just the ticket. Baldwin and O'Malley received traveling orders that would circle the midwest, attending bond drives and industrial incentive rallies from Michigan to Pennsylvania. They eventually found their way to Hollywood.

"We sold war bonds from Boston to California," O'Malley recalled. "Then we went on the Ginny Simms Show and came back to Washington. We were in different places, I can almost name them all, Ishpeming, Iron Mountain, Mackinaw, Sault Ste. Marie. Back down to the Twin Cities, Menominee, Marinette. I can't recall everything." It was a whirlwind trip that finally ended in O'Malley's hometown. "They would put us into a state trooper's car and drive us to the next city and have a lunch or breakfast

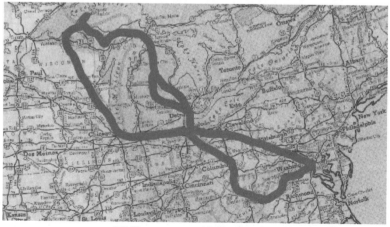

Mel's tour route 1943- Courtesy Beverly Baldwin

and make a speech, and finally we ended up with the commandant here in Chicago."

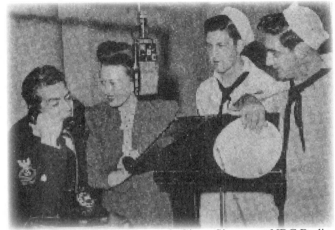
Mel and Ray with Vic Mature & Ginny Simms on NBC Radio

The men retold their story to countless radio interviewers and even more newspaper reporters. Family members from those lost on the *Esky* pleaded for details on their loved ones, and many times O'Malley admitted he just made things up. He did not know the crew nearly as well as Mel Baldwin but felt the lost sailor's families deserved kind remarks.

The entire crew were honored when Ray O'Malley and Mel Baldwin wrapped up their bond drive tour, returning for a ceremony that gave Purple Hearts to the men of the *Escanaba*. Ray remembers representing the crew during the ceremony. "Their next of kin got the medal.. and the

Mel Baldwin addresses the crowd during a rally

ATTENTION EVERYBODY!

You are invited to attend

FIVE GREAT

SAFETY And PATRIOTIC MEETINGS

Tuesday Night - Aug. 24 - OMAR Store Porch
Wed. Night - Aug. 25 - STIRRAT Store Outdoors
Thurs. Night - Aug. 26 - Rossmore Store Porch
Friday Night - Aug. 27 - Earling Store Porch P. M.
Sunday - Aug. 29 - 3:00 - p. m., Norton Store

BAND CONCERTS by Omar Boys Band
(Under Direction - CARL McELFRESH)

Special Addresses by
TWO MEMBERS OF THE
U. S. NAVY
Only Two Survivors Of The
"ESCANABA"
Sunk In Action In The
North African Waters

Let's all attend!
HEAR ABOUT THE EXPERIENCES
OF THESE TWO HEROES

Mine safety meeting poster- courtesy Beverly Baldwin

commandant said 'now everybody on board now has the purple heart.' By him giving the purple heart to them, it's like saying everyone of them are heroes."

O'Malley would never forget his crew-mates. Every June thirteenth he would light a candle at the local cathedral, where he bought a memorial walkway brick for the crew. Without fail he attended every memorial for the *Escanaba* in Grand Haven, Michigan, the ship's first homeport. "I missed a few parades, but never a memorial service. I guess I feel I owe it to the 101 men who are gone. I owe it to them to honor me. They were with me during some trying times. Ya know you can't sit here sixty years later and talk about Boot, Eddie, Boats, Prause, Peterson- I recall some of the names.. Arrighi.. the names come back occasionally."

Memorial at Grand Haven, MI

Ray only remembers seeing Mel Baldwin one more time, at the annual memorial in Michigan. Grand Haven now has a permanent memorial for the *Esky*, using the mast that was removed when the ship was converted at Manitowoc. A life raft also adorns the jack-staff, and a plaque that remembers the men.

Baldwin himself returned to Grand Haven aboard the *Escanaba's* sister ship, *Tahoma*. He did not re-enlist, instead he worked for the railroad and then joined the Air Force on December 29th, 1949. He served as a rescue specialist, working to recover downed pilots aboard speedboats. Mel served in Florida and then Okinawa,

Mel after the plane crash- Courtesy Beverly Baldwin

returning stateside in 1954. His wife Beverly said that he took up flying lessons using his GI Bill, money that is given to veterans to further their education. It was tough paying for flight time, so he was given free rent of a Piper Cub for chasing blackbirds from the corn and bean fields. He was flying low over the fields when he accidentally slammed into a canal bank. Mel's face, arms and left leg were injured and he lost sight in his left eye. Home movies later showed him next to the torn wreckage of the plane. Baldwin had once again cheated death, but this time was permanently scarred. He couldn't return to work and was discharged from the Air Force on October 18th, 1956, returning home to Staples with his wife.

Baldwin worked for a few years at an American Legion Club, and even survived a horrible car accident. Cancer would finally take Mel Baldwin in 1964. He was in for a routine checkup when they found the tumor in his abdomen. Eight inches of his intestine were removed, but the cancer spread and he passed away September 25th, 1964. His widow Beverly and their daughter Kelly Ann moved to the Pacific Northwest where they live today.

Ray O'Malley left the Coast Guard and joined the Chicago Police Department. His career included duty during the Chicago Riots, where he was hit by rocks and concrete. He was also involved in several big cases including the capture and trial of a cop killer in August, 1955, and the conviction of the men responsible for killing two postal inspectors in 1960.

A strange twist of fate put O'Malley once again aboard the tug that saved his life in World War II. A suspect materialized in the case of a murdered saloon keeper on State Street. He said detectives found similarities with the type of drink the suspect was ordering at local bars, and a trace on a long-distance phone call led the police on a chase that led all the way to a ship returning from Europe. Unaware the authorities were on to him, the ship was held

Baldwin and O'Malley- USCG photo

before anyone could disembark. Ray ran out to the vessel aboard a Coast Guard ship to apprehend the suspect. "We called the ship and said 'keep everybody aboard don't let anybody off.' And guess what ship took me to the freighter.. the *Raritan*!" Ray retired from the Chicago Police Department in 1979 as Acting Assistant Deputy.

Grand Haven started a memorial just two months after the *Escanaba* sank in 1943. A parade kicked off the bond drive designed to raise a million dollars, money designated to build a new *Escanaba*. It was the first of 64 memorials that Ray O'Malley would attend. The bond drive was successful and Escanaba II was commissioned on March 20th, 1946.

Michael & Ray O'Malley with author 2005- Ron Bloomfield photo

Ray attended his final *Escanaba* memorial in 2006. Lung cancer finally took the lone survivor on March 8th, 2007. His son Peter said he went peacefully after three days in the hospital. Together with his son Michael, Peter pledged to continue the O'Malley tradition of attending future memorials. On September 20th, Mike helped to carry out Ray's final wish to rejoin his crew. On the stern of the newest *Escanaba* (III), he and his father said their final goodbyes, and while taps was played aboard the cutter, they released Ray's ashes to the deep.

Mike O'Malley carries his grandfather's ashes

Burial ceremony aboard the *Escanaba III*, USCG Photos

O'Malley during the Chicago
Riots with Jesse Jackson

O'Malley watches the Black Panthers

THE CUTTER ESCANABA

Escanaba Launch-Bay County Historical Society

Launched in 1932 at Defoe Boat and Motor Works in Bay City, Michigan, the ship was stationed at Grand Haven, Michigan, and quickly took up the task of search and rescue. Among its accolades were the rescue of two downed airmail pilots; help in the rescue of the whaleback *Cort's* crew; and the 1934 emergency food delivery to the ice-bound residents of Beaver Island. This ship was far from just a 'festival favorite', and its capabilities for handling cold weather made it the right choice for polar duty when war broke out in Europe. During the 1940s it could be said that Greenland's main exports were cryolite and weather reports. Cryolite was found only in a few places around the world, and it was the

Cort stranded
Courtesy Canonie Research Library

106

best way to extract aluminum from bauxite ore. The area was also key for weather observations, as anything passing over this remote island would eventually affect Europe. The Nazis knew this and attempted several outposts of their own on the frozen continent. The United States moved to protect this area in 1941, establishing the Greenland Patrol to support the Army in building airbases in Greenland and to prevent German operations in the area. Thirteen installations were created, code named BLUIE bases.

The '*Esky*' was certainly designed for the icy region around the North Atlantic, but it was not quite a war ship. As World War II escalated, demand for 'weather patrols' brought several US ships into the region, and the *Escanaba* was slated for upgrade to a gunboat. This

Esky breaks ice in Michigan

involved several weeks at Manitowoc, Wisconsin, where one mast was removed and the other was repositioned. Space for several more crewmen was added and guns were mounted to the teak deck.

The attack on Pearl Harbor profoundly escalated the situation. In March of 1942 the *Esky* left the lakes, reporting for war at her new duty station on the Atlantic Ocean.

Some of the first enemy activity happened on June 15th, 1942. The *Escanaba* logged an underwater contact on its way from Cape Cod to Halifax and dropped several depth charges. Crew reported watching a German U-Boat breaking the surface and rolling over, but captured documents from the end of the war never showed a submarine lost in this area. Another contact was made at 6:20 p.m., and the *Escanaba* attacked, resulting in a large oil slick and a rush of air bubbles on the surface. Neither submarine was confirmed as lost by the German Navy. *U-Boat 87* was certainly in the area, because it attacked and sank the freighter *Port Nicholson* and tanker

Esky before conversion- B.C.H.S.

Cherokee that next day. The *Escanaba* rushed in to pick up thirty-nine survivors from the *Cherokee*. The freighter *Norlago* found only forty-four others of 160 who were onboard.

Escanaba crisscrossed the Atlantic several more times, escorting convoys between Nova Scotia, Sydney, Kungnat Bay and the Argentia Naval Base. Something happened to the cutter during one of these missions, as the *Esky* returned to Boston for repairs from December 5th until New Years Eve of 1942. It was here

Esky after conversion- Bay County Historical Society

that Mel Baldwin found time to run home and propose to Beverly. He expected to marry when the ship returned to Boston in June, but would return a hero even sooner.

The *Escanaba* left Boston and arrived at Argentia on January 2nd, making a run to Kungnat Bay and then returning to break ice in the harbor. Troop transports were more and more common in Greenland as construction crews arrived to build the BLUIE bases that surrounded the country. These bases would provide more than just security against the Nazis. Airplanes could now be flown from the factories in the United States to Europe via refueling stops in Greenland. But someone had to carve airports out of the land between the fjords, and it would take thousands of young recruits to do it. Benjamin Epstein was one of those new recruits, drafted after his senior year in business college to join the Army Air Corps. Only a few weeks later he was in administrator school in Denver, Colorado, where he met a new friend named Vincent Frucelli. The two would become inseparable, even attending Jewish worship services together, irregardless of the fact that Vince was a Catholic. Epstein says it was all part of being a buddy. "A buddy is like a loving brother who would do anything in the world for you, and you in turn would do the same for them."

Ben Epstein, *Dorchester* Survivor

The two buddies finished training and were sent via train to Maine, Massachusetts, and finally Staten Island, New York. Reporting to the docks for destinations unknown, Epstein didn't have much faith in the ship he was assigned to. "When war broke out, we didn't have any air transports or ship transports and so they dug up whatever ships they could. As long as it could float, I gather. And *Dorchester* was one of them."

Vincent Frucelli

Epstein had seen plenty of ships growing up in Brooklyn, but this would be his first trip on an ocean-liner. "Before we sailed I was walking on the inside deck and met a fifty year-old purser. I told him I'd never been on a ship this size and I want to know what I could eat to keep from getting ill. He said 'soldier, eat plenty of strawberry jam.' I asked him why and he said it will taste twice as good coming up as it does going down."

True to the purser's word, the trip was a rough one. Frucelli and Epstein were moved from the lower deck to a stateroom where all the unit's documentation was kept. The officer in charge felt the clerks should be with the paperwork, and it was a move that Epstein feels saved his life.

The troop ship tossed violently as it approached Canada, but it wasn't going to keep Frucelli from enjoying the legendary good chow onboard the *Dorchester*. "He ate enough for four men and then he said 'Ben, let me tell you what was on the menu.'" Epstein didn't want to hear about it, but his friend continued. As he described his meal, Frucelli began to change color. "When he finally turned green, he just made it to the sink and then crawled back to his bunk."

The 902 crew and passengers were pleased to finally touch ground in St. John's, Newfoundland, but it wasn't for long. Ben had just enough time to get a warm meal and shower and then was brought back to the *Dorchester*. The men and over a thousand tons of supplies and lumber were due in Narsarssuak, and they met up with the cutters *Tampa*, *Comanche* and *Escanaba* as escorts. Together with the merchant ships *Lutz* & *Biscaya*, Convoy SG-19 slowly made its way into the North Atlantic.

The good news was that the seas were much calmer for this part of the journey. The weather was clear and only a slight chop was found as the convoy neared Cape Farewell, Greenland. The bad news came from headquarters, which warned the convoy that enemy submarines were in the vicinity. Epstein remembers when

USAT Dorchester

Captain Hans Danielson told the crew and passengers about the U-boats. "On the evening of February 2nd, the captain of the ship spoke to us through the audio system. And he warned us, he said 'we are being followed by a German submarine; we are approximately ninety miles to Greenland. If we make it through the night, we will have air support from Greenland to bring us safely into port. But we have to make it through the night. And I urge you, sleep with every bit of clothing that you possess. Wear it, go to sleep with it. Everything, shoes, hat, gloves, life preservers, winter coat, everything. Wear it.' And he says, 'good luck.'"

At one in the morning, *U-223* fired its torpedoes at the convoy. A muffled explosion hit the *Dorchester* on the starboard side near the engine room, spewing ammonia gas into the air. Within three minutes, the captain ordered abandon ship, and the liner listed heavy to starboard. The ocean poured into the engine room, shutting the engines down.

All lights went out, and Vince and Ben felt their way through the blackness to the lifeboat station they were assigned to. It was one of the few boats that survived the explosion, as the number seven and number four lifeboats were unusable, damaged by fragments from the blast.

Epstein noticed that their lifeboat had already been deployed, and it was now bobbing in the ocean, tethered to the sinking ship by two cables. "I said I'm going to leap over the railing and catch that rope and I'm going to slide down to the lifeboat. Are you going to promise to follow and do exactly as I do?" Frucelli promised that he would follow, but after Epstein's descent he looked up and couldn't see his buddy. The lifeboat then collapsed from the sheer number of occupants that had sought refuge in it. Epstein went into the freezing water and instinctively swam away from the sinking ship. "One thing I knew from my reading is when a ship goes down it creates a suction, and it will drag everything down with it.. so off I went. I just swam."

On his lifejacket, a tiny red-colored flashlight automatically illuminated. Epstein was nearly overcome by the freezing water when he came upon a lifeboat. "I was cold, frozen and frightened. I tried to get in but couldn't. I told a soldier sitting on the edge, you've got to help me. If you don't, I'm going down."

Within twenty minutes of the explosion, *Dorchester* was settling stern first in the water. Lt. H.V. Stebbins, who wrote the report on the sinking, stated there was no panic on the deck. He believed that many did not know the severity of the situation. Part of that calmness came from four Army chaplains, who reportedly gave up their own lifejackets and gloves and stayed behind. Their sacrifice is legend today, remembered not only by the Immortal Chaplains

Foundation, but by several books and a documentary.

Epstein saw the ship's final moments from inside a lifeboat. "I saw the *Dorchester* making its last lurch into the ocean and it looked like a Christmas tree. Each (lifepreserver light) represented a soldier, a human being going down with the ship. I wished I could help them, but I couldn't."

The cutter *Comanche* had witnessed the explosion and immediately went to general quarters. Within six minutes of the sinking, the Escort Commander aboard the *Tampa* ordered the *Comanche* to locate and destroy the submarine. The *Tampa* took the remaining merchant ships to Skovfjord and returned to look for

Comanche- US Coast Guard Archives

survivors. *Escanaba* went in to look for survivors, a difficult task when an enemy U-Boat was known to be in the area. By 3:45, the *Comanche* had found a lifeboat while screening for the *Escanaba* and 40 survivors were brought aboard. *Escanaba* lowered its sea-ladders and readied its rubber-suited retrievers to look for survivors.

The 'retriever method' was credited to the crew of the *Escanaba*. It's executive officer, Lt. Bob Prause had practiced with the rubber suit off the dock at Bluie West one, looking for a better method of lifesaving after the *Cherokee* sinking. Ensign Richard Arrighi was the first in the water, jumping in to save a *Dorchester* survivor who fell out of the lifeboat. Two other Coast Guardsmen, Warren Deyampert and Forrest Rednour, also jumped in and grabbed men who were too frozen to help themselves. Rednour worked nearly four hours in the cold water, accounting for the most saves until his suit ripped and he had to come out. They brought in 50 sailors who appeared to be dead, but were revived by the ship's doctor, Asst. Surgeon Ralph Nix.

That is who greeted Ben Epstein when two *Escanaba* crewmen

plucked him from the lifeboat and brought him aboard the cutter. "He put me on a hard table and assigned five men to rub my body, feet, legs and arms. He told them to rub and don't dare stop. I know what they were worried about.. amputation."

Epstein slowly warmed under the constant attention of the crewmen. Dr. Nix took a flask of whisky and poured it down Epstein's throat. "What do you feel?" he asked. The *Dorchester* survivor could feel nothing. "Rub, rub, rub," Nix

Dr. Ralph Nix- courtesy Nix family

ordered. And finally Epstein's body started to respond. He told Dr. Nix that he was getting some feeling back in his extremities. "Finally I felt some tingling in my feet. Wow, what a feeling that was. I said 'Dr. Nix I think I have a little feeling down in my feet.' He bent down and hugged me. He was so thrilled it brought tears to my eyes. He was such a wonderful human being."

The *Escanaba* was originally designed to house sixty men, but was carrying nearly one hundred during wartime. That population swelled to over 230 when the *Dorchester's* crew came aboard. Mel Baldwin says people were stacked like cord wood inside. "We piled them under tables," he told a newspaper reporter. "They had to eat sitting on the men who were sleeping."

One hundred and forty-five victims were on board *Escanaba* by 9:30 in the morning. Thirteen were pronounced dead, with one hundred thirty-two survivors brought ashore when the cutter arrived in Narsarssuak on February 4th. Epstein, who had been stripped of his soaking wet clothes, walked ashore with only a blanket. *Comanche* brought back ninety-seven more survivors when it made port. *Tampa* searched the area but only found seven life rafts and two swamped lifeboats manned by corpses. *Tampa* returned to the base on February 6th.

Epstein would stay in Greenland for a year, working at Bluie West One and Bluie West 8.

Escanaba was soon back to convoy duty, but a trip to Argentia was interrupted when it apparently had an accident and required drydock repairs stateside. Mel Baldwin called his fiance in Staples, and on March 7th she hopped

Comanche's underwater resting place- S.Carolina DNR Photo

the next train to Boston. On March 10th, Beverly Bookhart became the bride of Melvin Baldwin at a ceremony performed by Judge Winkler. Dressed in a tan wool tweed suit with a corsage of orchids, Mrs. Baldwin said seven sailors were married that day in a mass celebration. Mel Baldwin's best man was an *Escanaba* crewman, Barton McCarty. The new couple had dinner at Boston's Adam's

Mel Baldwin

House, and Beverly Baldwin returned home to Minnesota.

Three months after the wedding, the *Escanaba* mysteriously exploded. Baldwin's best man was lost in the sinking, as were many of the rescue personnel who had saved the *Dorchester's* crew.

The news of the sinking hit especially hard to the men who had been saved by the cutter. Ben Epstein couldn't fight back the tears. "You can imagine what it did to us when we found out they were hit. These were our saviors! These beautiful human beings- saved our lives...lost."

The Coast Guard honored all of the crewmembers, especially Ensign Arrighi, Forrest Rednour and Warren Deyampert, who had risked their lives to save so many of the *Dorchester's* men. They were posthumously awarded the Navy and Marine Corps

Medal on August 18th, 1943. Lt. Cmdr. Peterson was awarded the Legion of Merit, and Lt. Robert Prause was awarded a Letter of Commendation for their jobs of organizing and supervising the rescues.

After the *Dorchester* rescues, Lt. Cmdr. Peterson submitted a request to honor the ship's doctor for his hard work. "We drifted down into a mass of survivors. The majority of the men were suffering from severe shock and exposure and couldn't climb up the sea ladder or the cargo nets, in fact, they couldn't even hang on to the lines thrown them. Retrievers in rubber suits were put into the icy water to recover the survivors. This system saved much valuable time and lives. By saving so much valuable time on each rescue operation, the ship

Escanaba's crew- USCG Archives

was able to contact that many more groups berfore the exposure could freeze them to death. Out of about fifty apparently dead men, only twelve were found to be dead by the ship's doctor, who worked valiantly with the assistance of members of the crew and survivors who had recovered, on those who showed signs of life. It is requested that Dr. Nix be commended for his splendid work with the rescuing of the 133 survivors from the *Dorchester*."

This request was honored with a commendation to Dr. Ralph Nix in 1943.

For meritorious services as Medical Officer of the Coast Guard

Cutter ESCANABA when that vessel rescued the survivors of a torpedoed U.S. transport on Feb. 3, 1943. When the Escanaba rescued about 133 survivors from the U.S. transport, Assistant Surgeon Nix ordered, directed and carried out the rendering of first aid to the survivors so skillfully and with such a high degree of efficiency that many men were saved who would otherwise have perished. The professional ability and devotion of duty displayed by Assistant Surgeon Nix on the occasion described reflects great credit upon the Naval Service.

The doctor was further honored when the Coast Guard named a medical clinic after him 50 years after his ship was lost on the Atlantic. Dedicated on June 13th, 1993, the Ralph R. Nix Clinic provides services at the training center in Petaluma, California.

The *Escanaba's* cook was also honored when a ship was launched in his honor. The *Rednour* was sponsored by his widow, launching on February 12th, 1945. It served in the battle for Okinawa, losing three sailors when it was hit by a kamikaze.

Theories about the sinking of the *Escanaba* continue to evolve even today. Author and former *Esky* II crewman James Carney, Jr. believes that it had to be a mine that sank the cutter, noting that all U-Boats were ordered out of the area by the spring of 1943. Ray O'Malley insisted it was a torpedo. "Think about it. How could a mine split a ship right in two? A mine would put a hole in it, but the *Escanaba* broke right in two. I saw the bow coming at me and the stern coming at me and I was blown up. I don't believe it was a mine. It was a torpedo."

Mel Baldwin's official statement seems to agree with O'Malley. In 1943 he told investigators -*In my opinion the damage at the time the ship was sunk and the sounds that I heard is that we were struck by a torpedo that was meant for the transport instead of our ship, and that we had just accidentally gotten into the line of fire.* Escanaba was the ninety-nineth of over 500 ships lost by the U.S. during World War II. In 2003 a Coast Guard history newsletter called the *Cutter* (**Newsletter 12 Autumn 2003**) hinted at an investigation at the wreck-site, located ninety-two miles from Ivigtut (in some 3000 meters of water), but nothing has been confirmed as of this writing.

Escanaba after launch in Bay City, MI- Bay Co. Historical Society

Crew shots from the *Escanaba*- US Coast Guard

Leonard Gabrysiak:

Wheelsman of the *Cedarville*

Len Gabrysiak aboard ship

Chapter Four- Brothers of the Sea

Wheelsman Leonard Gabrysiak grew up in Rogers City, a maritime community in northern Lower Michigan that was home to the world's largest limestone quarry. Calcite is so large that it can be seen from outer space, a 7-kilometer long bright white spot next to

Rogers City from 200 miles up- ISS Photo NASA

Loading limestone- author's collection

the top of Lake Huron.

Michigan Limestone opened the quarry in 1911, carving out the landscape to reveal 500 million year old seashells that had solidified into calcium carbonate rock. This area was once underwater, covered by a shallow sea during the Paleozoic era. Today these ancient creatures are practically 'white gold', used in everything from purifying sugar and steel, to constructing buildings and roadways. Michigan Limestone needed a way to move this stone after it was dynamited from the ground and crushed to a manageable

Carl D. Bradley- Great Lakes Lore Museum

size. In 1912 the steamer *Calcite* was built, followed by the *W.F. White, John G. Munson* and *Myron C. Taylor*. In 1925 the electrically propelled *T.W. Robinson* was launched, but the Bradley Transportation Company's true crowning moment came two years later. The largest cargo carrier on the lakes arrived in Calcite on July 28th, 1927.

Named for the president of Michigan Limestone & the Bradley Transportation Company, the *Carl D. Bradley* would reign as 'Queen of the Lakes' for several years. At 630 feet long, it was a giant, capable of hauling record-breaking loads.

Len Gabrysiak joined the Bradley fleet in 1951, first working in the galley on the *Bradley*. Another crewman fell ill and he was moved to deckhand, where he spent a lot of time in and around the ship's cargo hold. "I didn't really care for her, I thought she was ugly." Gabrysiak said, "Her after cabins sure didn't do justice to her, in my opinion."

It was down below that Gabrysiak learned about the stress put on the ships in heavy seas. Water often accumulates in the bottom of the ship during stormy ventures, and one of his jobs was to pump that water back into the lake. To help with this procedure, the ship can be trimmed with ballast water so the stern rides lower than the bow, letting gravity move the leaking water to where they could pump it out.

Returning empty from Gary, Indiana, the *Bradley* would pump lake water into its ballast tanks to ride lower in the waves. "We were down in the tunnel sumping out the water," Gabrysiak recalled, noting that every groan of the ship can be heard in the tunnels, which is unnerving for many who go below. "Cripe, I hear SSSHHHHHH. What is that? Ah, it's water coming out of the side tank rivets." But it was the ricochet sounds that really made him wonder about the ship's integrity. "Every once in a while you'd hear PING. What's that? Probably a rivet... breaking off.'"

Those rivets literally held the ship together. Gabrysiak found that these stressed 'missiles' would fly off and end up in the cargo hold bottom. "I did find out when you shovel out the spillage, in all that dirt you'd see a few rivet heads there." The flying rivets made him think twice about staying below in a storm. "I made it a point- the only time in the tunnel was when I had to work down there."

The youngest of six kids, Len Gabrysiak grew up on south First Street in a section of Rogers City dubbed 'Polish Town'. Tragedy would not only take his mother early in his life, but also his brother. "Frank was 27 years old on the *EY Townsend*," Gabrysiak remembered, "They had loaded in Duluth and four to five hours out they called Frank for his watch and he wasn't there. They searched the whole ship and he was nowhere to be found. They notified the Coast Guard and they made a search and didn't find anybody."

Gabrysiak's oldest brother Stanley was actually the first to work the lakes as a sailor, and he was hurt while sailing for Bradley Transportation. "In 1937 they had an explosion on the *W.F. White*. He was stokerman and he went down into the bilge as far as he could to get away from the steam. He still got burned- not real bad, but pretty good. One or two lives were lost, they were scalded to death."

The loss of his mother put extra duties on the youngest Gabrysiak. "When I was home, my dad and I were living alone and I had to do all the shopping, cooking, washing, cleaning. I never had much time to myself." He would tease his father about how much he would be missed when he went to the boats. "I used to sing a little song to my dad; 'one of these days, now don't forget it.. one of these days you're gonna regret it.' I'd go on and on. He said, 'I know what you're thinking... you don't like it here.' I didn't. But I didn't tell him that."

Len grew up frustrated that he couldn't recall anything about his mother, who died when he was just a year and a half old. "I thought, how come I can't remember my mother? If I could just get an image of her face." He finally built up enough courage to ask his father about her during a game of rummy. "I asked him, how come you never remarried? He looked at me and said 'There was only one woman in my life and that was your mother.' And that was that."

123

By 1954, the quarry was owned by U.S. Steel and it was at the apex of production, shipping 15 million tons in one year. Gabrysiak worked on nearly all of the Bradley boats, and he tried several different jobs aboard ship. He certainly knew where he didn't want to work. "I think I was on the *Robinson* as a wiper. I didn't care for the engine room. It seemed like they were down there scrubbing all the time. I didn't like that."

A Bradley boat utilizes its self-unloading boom

Gabrysiak got his required sailing hours in and took the test for Able Bodied Seaman. "I decked for a year and went to St. Ignace and wrote for my A-B. I thought it would be an easy deck watch job- sound the tanks- but it wasn't that easy. You still had to go on the dock and handle cables. I waited a year and a half to get a deck watch job."

After time aboard the *Calcite,* Gabrysiak moved to the *Clymer* and finally the *Myron C. Taylor,* where he spent his free time learning

124

how to steer the ship. The company was also expanding their cargoes to include trips to new ports. "We also got raw iron ore out of Escanaba on the *Taylor*. That was a new thing, we mostly did stone and coal mainly. When pellets started coming, self-unloaders could move in. Straight-deckers needed Hullet unloaders. Now they've eliminated the Hullets, made them all self unloaders."

The self-unloaders were also the perfect solution to a huge building project in the straits. "In the fifties I was hauling into the Mackinac Bridge. Where Stone Port is now, they built the caissons and put them on barges and hauled them up to Mackinac by tug. When we went up with a load of stone, they had people on the catwalk of the caisson. I was on the boom one time and the weather kicked up. We had big waves rolling in there. It was a hassle to get situated."

Len made seven trips to the bridge well before any of the superstructure was raised. The massive caissons would eventually become supports for the towers, which stood 45 stories tall. The stone plant would wash down the stone several times, then repeat the cleaning process aboard ship before it was dumped into the caissons. "We'd dump 12-14,000 tons of stone and you can't even see where it went. It would be a big pile on the deck, but not in those caissons!"

Mackinac Bridge's caisson ready for concrete

By 1955 the caissons were down to bedrock, filled with limestone and cement. And as rough as it could get on the freighters, Len knew it was worse working on the Mackinac Bridge. "I seen a time late in the fall and as the caisson was driven down and they added a new section to it, welded. The spray hit their rain gear and ice would fall off.. and I said boy them guys are earning their money! I seen it myself. That water would hit and it would freeze and when they'd bend, it would break off."

In 1956, there was a shortage of men with AB licenses, and Len's deferment from military service was almost guaranteed. He knew he was eligible for the draft until he was 35, so he opted to serve his country while he was still 'young.' His notice came and he was off to the Army, training at Fort Lewis, Washington, and Selfridge Field near Detroit. As Private First Class Gabrysiak, he would be assigned to a missile site in Utica, Michigan.

Promotions in the service did not seem to come fast enough and Len opted to leave the Army after two years and return to the lakes. A slow down in the limestone trade that summer laid off many of his friends and idled several ships including the *Carl D. Bradley.*

Aerial view of Calcite- Michigan Limestone Collection

Gabrysiak shipped out late that summer on the *Myron C. Taylor,* and by mid-November, he heard the *Bradley* was coming out of

126

the 'frog pond' for a few fall runs. The wheelsman remembers November 18th, 1958 vividly.

"We loaded stone out of here for Algoma Steel just beyond the Soo locks. We had just left the Soo locks and a whole gale come up, you could just see the waves pounding over the dock, where we were supposed to unload." The *Taylor* went to anchor to wait out the storm and Len went up to the pilothouse to relieve the helm for dinner. "We're at anchor!" the captain exclaimed, wondering why the ship needed someone on the wheel when they were not underway. Len felt it was a ploy to keep him from overtime, but

Bradley heading for another load of limestone- Michigan Limestone Collection

he knew the contract, and the on-duty wheelsman went aft for supper. "I just whistled a tune.. let him moan and groan. The wheelsman comes back and says, 'Gabby, Gabby.. the *Bradley's* sinking in Lake Michigan! It's breaking up.. it's on the radio.. mayday, mayday.. holy cripe!'"

The *Bradley* was returning from its usual run to the steel mills near Gary, Indiana when it encountered 30-foot seas on Lake Michigan. Crossing the top of the lake, they took on the seas that raced up the lake from the southwest. Sixty mile per hour winds screamed

127

through the unloading boom as the deck split and the bow plowed into the water. Only two men survived- Elmer Fleming and Frank Mays.

Gabrysiak knew the senior officer that was found floating for 15 hours on a life-raft. He sailed with first mate Elmer Fleming back in 1951, taking the *White* up through the St. Lawrence with a load of coal.

The Captain of the *Taylor* also knew someone on board the *Bradley*, evidenced by the fact that he pulled up anchor in the storm and attempted to unload. "Eight o'clock he pulls up anchor and we go into Algoma. What a sight.. that boat took a banging against the dock. He come down on deck and told the watchman.. tell them to put all they can on the belts, whether it spills or not. We gotta get unloaded and get outta here!" Gabrysiak said the tossing boat made it impossible to neatly unload the stone. "The boom was way up like that.. next thing its down in the pile.. you couldn't control it."

The skipper apparently knew the conveyorman onboard the *Bradley*, and Gabrysiak thought the rush to unload was an attempt to get the *Taylor* down to Lake Michigan to help in the search. "When I came on watch, here we were at anchor and couldn't get out of there.. Munuscong Bay. There must have been 15-20 boats there waiting for the weather."

The captain ordered the wheelsman to weave around the sheltered fleet and make his way down to DeTour Light. The southwest winds that sank the *Bradley* were also whipping the top of Lake Huron into a frenzy. "The mate says 'Len you're going to have to hold her more up than that.' He keeps telling me just watch the magnetic and hold up what you have to keep her on course. With all that ballast she was dipping water to the starboard, almost to the deck. I thought he was going to go to Lake Michigan to look for the *Bradley* survivors, and I thought if he makes a haul towards that bridge I'm getting a lifejacket on. And he can go, cuz I'm leaving. I'll get off of here."

Sailor Ed Brewster remembers the storm aboard the steamer *Calcite*. "We were in Saginaw Bay when it sank. Five in the afternoon, I had my radio on and I was in my room and the newscast said a ship was in distress in Lake Michigan. I could get ship to shore calls, and I heard the office calling and they must have told him it was the *Bradley*, and they told us to take precautions."

Gabrysiak didn't think they were taking many precautions as they headed around the Upper Peninsula towards Rogers City. "We come around Calcite and that breakwall.. man, it was blowing, did she take the dips. Finally one hatch cover came off and bent the leaves all to hell, and they had to take a crane at the dock and lift them all out. The shop bent them all back in place and the old man left the boat. The First mate, Doc Monroe, had never skippered- but he had his master's license, so he moved up. We left Calcite for Erie, Pennsylvania."

November 22nd was proclaimed an official day of mourning for the community of Rogers City, dedicated to the thirty-three men who lost their lives. Funerals were held at several local churches, and the gymnasium near St. Ignatius church held nine of the caskets. At noon all work stopped for the US Steel fleet and memorial services were held aboard. Gabrysiak was part of the commemoration aboard the *Taylor*. "We went up town and he ordered a flower wreath, said prayers and tossed in the wreath in Erie."

The *Myron C. Taylor* steamed up the Detroit River and the crew was eager to buy newspapers from the mailboat to get any details they could on their friends. "In Detroit we came up to the *Wescott* and everyone wanted to get the paper hoping there would be something about the *Bradley* and there was. Big headline, Sunk in Lake Michigan, lots of loss of life and they were going to have a fund, and I guess every boat in the fleet was contacted for donations for *Bradley* relief. I was first.. I gave 50 bucks to start it out.. that was a lot!"

Questions arose not only over the condition of the *Bradley*,

Bradley liferaft aboard *Sundew*

which was due for dry-dock repairs in Manitowoc, but also about why the *Bradley's* skipper, Captain Roland Bryan didn't seek shelter like so many others did. Gabrysiak said there certainly were questions aboard his boat. "Mostly, everyone was wondering why were they out there? A lot of others were at anchor. Maybe it was a tonnage bonus, I don't know."

Captain Bryan, along with fourteen others, was never found. Watchman Frank Mays, who survived on the liferaft with first mate Fleming, told investigators he heard a loud THUD and immediately climbed the ladders to the pilothouse.

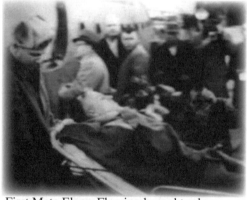
First Mate Elmer Fleming brought ashore

"When I was there, someone said to get the liferaft ready.. so I did," Mays explained to the author in a 1995 interview. He watched the bow sink as he rode the liferaft down, finally being thrown from it as a giant wave swept him off the ship. Mays surfaced right next to the raft and climbed back aboard in the storm. He then pulled Elmer Fleming aboard. They would be the only survivors from what would become Lake Michigan's largest shipwreck. Fleming eventually returned to the lakes on another ship, but Mays elected to keep his feet on dry land.

Fleming eventually returned to another pilothouse, becoming captain on the *W.F. White, Cedarville* and *Calcite II*. Ed Brewster remembers being in a gale with Fleming in the pilothouse. "I remember we left with a load of dolomite and he took the *Calcite*

Ed Brewster

II right out into the storm and the next morning he said it was the worst storm he had seen since the *Bradley*."

Ed started with the Bradley boats in 1956 after a four-year stint in the Navy. That experience paid off, as he soon had his AB and was deckwatch on the *Cedarville*. "I wheeled for Elmer Fleming on the *Cedarville*. He was a real nervous person and no one ever asked him about (the sinking). He was a relief captain of the *Cedarville* but wasn't aboard it when it sank."

Mystery surrounds Fleming's final trip to the *Cedarville*. Len Gabrysiak remembers it was during a blinding snowstorm that dumped over a foot of snow in Rogers City. "Good Friday, Elmer Fleming came out and put his bags on the dock and told the deckhand to take them up to his room. He did, and (Fleming) left the boat. Fifteen minutes later he came back to the dock and told the watchman to have the deckhand go get his bags; he was getting off. He got his bags and left the ship. I don't know if he was in contact with the office or not, but there must have been some kind of communication there."

Captain Fleming left the ship in March of 1964, never to return. Len could only speculate that it was the storm that ended his career so abruptly. "Well everybody thought he had a relapse from the *Bradley*.. the bad weather, he didn't want to go out. He had been in the freezing rain or snow before. That's what everybody thought."

Without Captain Fleming, the first mate, Martin Joppich, moved up to skipper and Harry Peichan jumped from second to first mate. The change in rank also affected Stanley Rygwelski, who moved to the second mate position. The only other licensed officer aboard the *Cedarville* was the newly-papered Leonard Gabrysiak. Len would leave the wheel to become third mate. "We left Calcite, I was kind of nervous, ya know. What in the hell kind of break-in was this? First trip of the season... storm, well... I come on watch at Forty-Mile Point at eight o'clock and Joppich says, 'lay out a

course through Cheboygan channel.' I told him we couldn't go through there, as we didn't even know if *Mackinaw* (the icebreaker) was out."

Mackinaw- Gulau Collection

Gabrysiak said he told Joppich of a better route to the north. "I said it might be better to go around Round Island between Mackinac Island so if we get caught in ice, at least she won't go up on the shoals, so we went around." That journey was going to be longer than expected, and as Second Mate Stanley Rygwelski came to the pilothouse at noon, the *Cedarville* came to an abrupt stop. "Stanley came in and I told him what was happening and just as soon as I did- there we were, stopped in the ice. Couldn't go any

M/V Cedarville

further."

Cedarville was a 588-foot freighter first launched in 1927 as the *A.F. Harvey,* built at the same yard which would turn out the massive *Edmund Fitzgerald* some 30 years later. The *Harvey* sailed for Pittsburgh Steamship until 1952 when it joined the Bradley fleet. It was converted into a self-unloader at Bay City, Michigan, over the winter of 1956. *Cedarville* received its unique streamlined smokestack when its boilers were replaced five years later. It was a powerful ship but no match for early season ice in the straits. Gabrysiak knew they would need the massive Coast Guard cutter *Mackinaw* to break them free. "The old man was up there so we shut the engines off and we called *Mackinaw.* They were at the dock. We said 'this is the *Cedarville..* we're stuck in the ice. Need some assistance.' They said 'stay where you are, we'll come out 8 o'clock in the morning.' So we backed up, dropped both hooks and they came out and broke us out to Lake Michigan. So we made that trip and came back to Calcite."

Ed Brewster had spent his last seven seasons aboard the *Cedarville*, opting for its newly renovated living spaces over the ancient *Calcite*. He had many friends on board, including Captain

Joppich. "We had a real good crew and got along great with the captain. He was a nice person, I wheeled for him." In fact, Brewster had wheeled the ship right back into port the midnight of May 7th, 1965. But the subsequent arrival of the *W.F. White* brought some changes to the command line-up on the *Cedarville*. Charles Cook left the *White* to take on the *Cedarville's* third-mate job, which bumped Len Gabrysiak back to wheelsman, and Ed Brewster would go back to watchman.

Gabrysiak made a quick trip home to his wife Pat, but planned to return around 3 a.m.. Brewster would also get to see his wife Jean, but only for a few early hours. He was scheduled to clean up the deck after loading stone at four in the morning. "We left at about five in the morning and I worked until eight and went right to bed. It was about a five hour run from Rogers to the bridge."

Cedarville carried a variety of cargos, but most of her dents in the cargo hold were caused by countless tons of limestone. Over fourteen-thousand tons of the largest chunks, called open hearth, filled the ships belly on this run to Gary. Thick fog enveloped the ship, a mist that would get even more blinding as the day wore on.

Local newspapers reported several accidents because of that fog. The steamer *J.E. Upson* crashed into the Grays Reef Lighthouse in Lake Michigan, and the *D.C. Everest* and *Bethlehem Steel Company* were aground near the Soo due to the fog. Sixty-five ships were bottlenecked in the harbor waiting for their chance to go through the locks, and the *Ashcroft* also had left the channel and was stranded. The *Ashcroft* knew well the dangers of limited visibility, having been damaged after a foggy crash that sank the *James Reed* on Lake Erie on April 27th, 1944.

Despite countless accidents that have occurred in foggy conditions, few ships were slowing down. The German freighter *Weissenburg's* boatswain, Peter Hahn, was surprised when another foreign ship overtook them two miles from the Mackinac Bridge. "We were on the way back from Chicago. We delivered our cargo

Weissenburg- Courtesy Peter Hahn

and we hit bad fog. I could hear foghorns all over and could hear a ship close to us. It was the *Topdalsfjord*, under a Norwegian flag, and she was that close to us. (She was) Going much faster than we did. And then she disappeared, and at 8 a.m. my watch was over and I had breakfast with my buddies and relaxed in my cabin."

The *Cedarville* was approaching the Mackinac Bridge from the east, running at full speed, near twelve knots. Blinded by thick fog, Len Gabrysiak could tell neighboring traffic simply by the sound of their engines. "I hadn't been on watch too long when we went by the Cheboygan traffic buoy and you could hear chug, chug. There's one of those Ford boats- you could hear it by those diesels just a chuggin'. And I can see her faintly through the fog. They were blowing whistle to take her on the port side." Sound was hardly the best way to know if traffic was approaching in the cloak of clouds that hugged the cool waters. *Cedarville* used radar to look ahead for danger, fixing its position from returns on the screen and radio signals from the RDF antennae.

The *SS Benson Ford* had set up a 'passing arrangement' with the *Cedarville*, agreeing verbally via the radio and with a single blast of the horn, that the ships would pass each other on the port side.

135

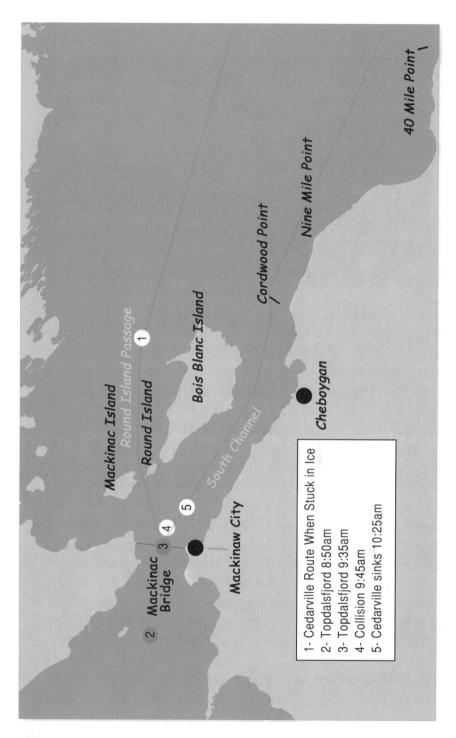

Mackinac Island
Round Island Passage

Round Island

1

Bois Blanc Island

Cordwood Point

Nine Mile Point

40 Mile Point

Cheboygan

South Channel

Mackinac Bridge
2
3
4
5

Mackinaw City

1- Cedarville Route When Stuck in Ice
2- Topdalsfjord 8:50am
3- Topdalsfjord 9:35am
4- Collision 9:45am
5- Cedarville sinks 10:25am

136

Cedarville's pilothouse was buzzing with activity. Third Officer Charlie Cook was fixed to the ship's RCA radar screen, which returned generic 'blips' that indicated other ships around them. Radio calls and visual identification were the only way to indicate 'who was who.' Today freighters send out radio identification, much like airplane transponders, to tell who they are and where they are going. That morning Third Mate Cook only had a series of moving dots to decipher a course for the *Cedarville* to travel.

Now just a few miles from the congested passage of the Mackinac Bridge, Captain Joppich hailed one of the 'blips' to find it was the *Weissenburg*. Again, a port-to-port passing was agreed upon, with Captain Werner May aboard the *Weissenburg* opting for a transit to the south channel. At 9:38 a.m., the German ship slipped underneath the bridge, warning the *Cedarville* that a Norwegian ship was in front of them.

"Then after that, a lot of strange things started to happen. Change course here, change there, then somebody showed up. Change the course, steady there. Call another boat and it won't answer." Gabrysiak recalled that the skipper tried to hail the mystery ship on the radio. "There's a boat out there that won't answer. Next thing- there's she's coming. Out of the fog. Cook is at the radar he says, 'Jeeze Captain, she's closing in on us!' I looked over there and forty-five degrees I can see the bow out of the fog. That's it.. we're going to get hit. Put her hard left.. trying to swing around. Too late."

Gabrysiak would later report to investigators that the *Cedarville* never reduced speed until their course was turned to the right at 325 degrees. Captain Joppich told investigators that the ship was at half-speed at this time, sounding the horns for a port-to-port passing.

The *Topdalsfjord* was making 17 knots as it passed the *Weissenburg* and approached the bridge. When their radar indicated the *Cedarville* was about a mile and a half ahead, the ship checked

137

down to dead slow. Captain Rasmus Haaland would later say the limited visibility made him opt to turn left for Round Island, and he reported to investigators that his radioman did announce their intentions over the radio. The captain stated that he realized the two ships were converging and signaled his engine room for emergency full reverse.

The *Topdalsfjord's* bow sliced into the *Cedarville's* left side, below the waterline near the number seven hatch. The ship wedged in for only a moment and was spun clear from the forward momentum of the *Cedarville*. Captain Joppich ordered all stop and Gabrysiak

Topdalsfjord- Courtesy Peter Hahn

immediately thought of the men who were off duty. "I thought 'you gotta get the crew out of their quarters.' Well he got on the phone right away, he wanted to talk to Parilla."

The voice that answered Joppich's radio call told him that his boss, Joseph Parilla, was in Pittsburgh. Gabrysiak didn't wait for him to finish his conversation on the phone. "I said, 'you gotta go ring the general alarm.' He says 'you go ring the general alarm.' So I rang the general alarm. There were people sleeping and I didn't know how bad it was."

The wheelsman glanced around the pilothouse and realized there weren't any lifejackets nearby. He asked the skipper for permission to leave his station. "Request permission to leave the pilothouse to get lifejackets." 'Go ahead.'" Gabrysiak made the trip quickly. "It didn't take me long to go down and get the lifejackets. The Coast Guard had condemned the old ones in the spring, and the new ones weren't put in the rack yet so I grabbed three and that's the last time I saw Stanley Haske."

Len had a brief conversation with his fellow wheelsman. "He asked me, 'What are you going to do Len?' I said, 'Gee I don't know, Stan. I gotta get back to the pilothouse' and I was back in a flash. I put (my lifejacket) on right away. Joppich and Cook threw theirs down on the deck."

The sudden jolt of the impact brought Ed Brewster out of a deep slumber. "I felt the impact of the collision, it woke me right up. I was sleeping pretty sound but it woke me right up. Then the bells went off and the first mate came down and told us all to get our lifejackets on. We all did that and went to the collision tarp from the boom and put it over the hole."

Bob Bingle was also off duty, but a fellow watchman ran down to his cabin to make sure he was awake. "Time of the collision I was sleeping and my roommate, Art Furman, said we were about to get hit so I jumped up and put my lifejacket on. I don't know where I went- I guess back in my room and we got hit, but you just felt a thud. It was so foggy on deck we couldn't see them, but we got the crash tarp out and we went back and dropped that over, but the hole was so big it just went straight through. Art was in his rain gear and I said, 'get out of your rain gear!' He said, 'no, we're not going to sink.'"

Most of the crew believed this to be true. Of the three survivors the author has interviewed, each said there was no panic. The Straits of Mackinac are only a few miles wide, more like the Mississippi River than a Great Lake. Each man thought the ship would certainly make it to shore, they just weren't sure which shore Joppich would pick.

And while there was not panic in the wheelhouse, Gabrysiak said there certainly was confusion, especially as the captain radioed WLC to connect him with Joseph Parilla, the manager of operations for the fleet. "We're still at anchor and he's calling the office. 'We have a situation here we've been hit in the fog.' And

Topdalsfjord bow damage- Courtesy Roger LeLievre

I'm taking this all in, watching the time and everything. Pretty soon he's asking Parilla, 'Do you think I should beach her?' Or Parilla must have said, 'Can you beach her?' 'Well beach her, I don't know.'"

Joppich had little more than a few weeks of experience as captain of the *Cedarville*, and he certainly never experienced anything like this. Gabrysiak believes most of the decision making was coming remotely. "The way it seemed to me was like Parilla was telling him what to do and he didn't even know what the hell the circumstances were, because he's not there. I thought to myself 'well Martin.. you're the master.. you know what the situation is.. you've got to make the decision. Don't ask someone out there someplace else. YOU make the decision.' But that's for me to say."

The *Cedarville's* number two hold was quickly filling with water, listing the vessel to the port side. "When we first got hit we took on a hell of a list to port," Gabrysiak said. "She was over there maybe thirty-seven degrees, I'd say- a long way. And I said if you don't compensate for that list, she's going to roll over." The skipper ordered him to take care of the problem with a telephone call to engineering. " 'Well call the engine room and tell them to compensate for that list.' That's what I did, and he was still on the phone trying to get a hold of some of these boats or whatever was going on there."

Captain Joppich radioed the *Weissenburg*, requesting the name of the Norwegian ship. *Weissenburg* replied and offered assistance, to which Joppich refused. Captain May had already loaded his men into the *Weissenburg's* lifeboats, and he went on the loudspeaker to recall his men. Peter Hahn remembers the callback. "I was in the starboard lifeboat and cleared it and gave the order to swing the boats out. And then (The captain) dismissed the call and he said, 'It's over, the captain of the *Cedarville* said they'd try to beach the ship.' So we went back and the captain said, 'leave the boats the way they are.'"

Joppich's decision to run towards Mackinaw City worried the wheelsman, who felt Bois Blanc Island was closer. "Well, whatever Parilla said.. (Joppich) told the watchman to go down and heave up the anchor. Well they had a hell of a time, the anchor was hung up, and then they had to back her up and finally broke free and got the anchor up. Next thing I heard something about

Charlie Cook, something about the radar, to lay out a course there over on the Mackinaw side. I couldn't see because they have the hood off the radar now. I just do my job- keep her on the course that they tell me."

The ship continued to shudder and settle into Lake Huron. Joppich knew it was finally time to admit he needed help. He ordered the engines stopped and the rudder amidships. Gabrysiak asked permission to lock open the pilothouse doors. "I said, I ain't getting trapped in here.. no way. Finally he says, 'That's it. Mayday, mayday this is the *Cedarville*. We're sinking.' I went out on the port side, by this time we were compensated for the list, leveled off. And I could still see the deck."

Gabrysiak grew more concerned as Lake Huron started washing over the front of the ship. "The bow and the foc'sle was covered with water already, and I saw a life ring and I said that baby is coming with me right now."

Bob Bingle was already on deck, readying their escape. "We swung the lifeboats out and were awaiting further orders which we never did get a abandon ship. Fog was lifting a bit and we could see forward end from aft, and the bow went under and the ship just rolled."

Ed Brewster made it to the starboard life raft when *Cedarville* nosed under, rolling to starboard as it

Bob Bingle

sank in one hundred feet of water. "I was standing in the lifeboat and Casey [Jones] came out of the engine room and said, 'Wait for me.' I held out my hand and said, 'Here I'll help you' and just then a huge wave came down the deck and that's the last I remember." Eugene "Casey" Jones was never seen again. The wave of water swept him from the deck and caused Bob Bingle to plunge into the thirty-seven degree water. "I grabbed a porter, Larry Richards, and ran across the coalbunker and dove in. When I came up the forward raft was six feet away. As I was climbing on board, the second mate was coming up the other side of the raft, and we got aboard and seven or eight fellas ended up on the raft."

The starboard lifeboat would be dragged down with the ship, but the port boat swung over as the *Cedarville* rolled, taking stockerman Billy Holley with it. Ed Brewster would notice after rescue that Billy's carton of cigarettes were dry. "I said, 'What happened to you, you didn't even get wet.' He said 'No, I rode the port lifeboat right over the ship.' I don't know how he did it, but he did it."

The crew on the *Weissenburg* heard the mayday and were scrambling back to their life boats. Peter Hahn remembered hearing the alarm bell once again. "I was just back at the mess hall and all the sudden the alarm sounded again. *To the lifeboats, to the lifeboats, she sunk.* I rushed to my station. There were three men in our lifeboat, and when I looked to the starboard side from our bow I could see a big water fountain, water shooting fifteen to twenty feet up in the air. That was from the air that came out of the *Cedarville*."

The Germans were in the water moments after the sinking, picking up survivors within twenty minutes of going into the water. Billy Holley's boat would eventually contain the first mate, Elmer Emke, Tony Rosmys, and Mike Idalski. The life raft, which floated free when the ship sank, would mean salvation for the second mate, Ed Brewster, Art Martin, Bob Bingle and conveyor man Ron Piechan.

Len Gabrysiak, gripping his life ring as he plunged into the lake, sank deeper than he wanted into the freezing water. "Felt like I got tangled up for a while, and then I was going right down. The water was like through my eyelids.. you know.. I could see through the skin.. water was light then dark.. pitch black. I mean black. I was going down, down, down. I could tell I was going down just by the suction. It seemed I was going down fast!"

His death-grip on the life ring was stressed beyond his strength as the buoyancy of the float fought to bring him back to the surface. "I held my hand around my lifejacket and put my other hand on that life ring and finally the pressure was so strong my whole hand just opened up and there went the life ring. And by that time I had settled pretty much from going down any further and then I thought, geez, I'm in that under tow."

The straits have unique fast currents that have become feared by many who have to work near the water. "I remember when they built that bridge they were talking about that under tow. Never found a few guys that got into that under tow and they are constantly moving and they'll never find them. I said 'God, if I get in there, I'm not going up.'" Gabrysiak's days at St Ignatius Catholic School taught him to turn to prayer. "I said five Hail Marys, starting from when I went down till the surface when I hit the collision block. That oak block right there in my chest.. ohhh.. I shot clear out of the water.

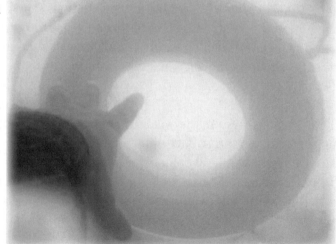

144

My upper body was right out of the water and right back down."

Gabrysiak saw the life raft, but the current kept him from getting to it. He tried to keep his circulation moving, but found it difficult as hypothermia set in. He whistled but didn't think the boat heard him. "Finally I saw them coming my way and I started screaming. I barely got my hands over the gunnel and that's all I remember. That's when Peter Hahn told he got me in the lifeboat and I wanted to jump back into the water."

Hahn, who had quit school at age 14 to go to sea, says he knew exactly what the men were going through. His father was in the engine room when the *Willhelm Gustloff* was torpedoed during

Peter Hahn- Courtesy Peter Hahn

World War II. Hahn himself was shipwrecked twice; once when his ship ran on the rocks and the other in a collision with a Greek tanker. This time he was playing the role of rescuer. "We saw a lot of debris, we saw everything, we got by that and that's where we saw the first people that we tried to (save) and we got a little further- when we shut our engine off to hear those calling. We came closer, we picked another one up and he was in shock, screaming. He didn't know where he was. We had him in the boat and he tried to jump back into the lake. I believe he thought he was still on the *Cedarville*."

The crew grabbed a hold of Gabrysiak and brought him back to their ship, using their bell and the ship's whistle to rendezvous with the *Weissenburg*. Len was unconscious, but was told later about

145

how they revived him. "They got me aboard the *Weissenburg* and had to cut all my clothes off. They said I was all swollen up. I woke up.. first thing I asked, 'where am I?' All white room.. like a hospital room on the ship. I was shaking, I never shook so hard in my life. Hot water bottles were all the way down from my neck down to my feet. Four or five blankets on me, just shaking wild. They said, 'you're going to be all right Mr. Gabrysiak.'"

Wheelsman Stanley Haske was picked up by the *Weissenburg's* crew, barely clinging to life. "We had given him mouth to mouth, and my partner, who had to clean his mouth, said he bit his finger- so we thought he would make it. We worked really hard on him. We got him on the ship and into the shower to warm him up, but he didn't make it." The crew also brought deckwatchman Paul Jungman aboard, but he also died from exposure and asphyxiation.

Captain Joppich was found in the water, clinging to the life jacket that he never put on. Third Mate Charlie Cook was last seen trying to put on his life jacket in the wheelhouse.

In nearby Cheboygan, the Coast Guard cutter *Mackinaw* recalled its crew. Engineman third class Curt Anderson was downtown when he heard the horn of his ship calling. "The captain always said if there was an emergency when we were in port they would sound the whistle, and I remember I was up town and I could hear the whistle of the *Mackinaw* blowing and blowing and several of us on liberty mustered back to the ship to search

Curt Anderson- Courtesy Jay Cole

for the *Cedarville*."

Mackinaw left its homeport at 10:42 a.m., racing eighteen miles to the site of the sinking. "We got underway with a short-handed crew but enough to run the ship. That's the first time I had ever seen the *Mac* run at full speed ahead." Curt was called to the galley as part of the rescue detail. "As we were enroute to the search site, we were briefed, and they picked a crew for the motor lifeboat which included me. We made a boat ready for launch and the captain showed us a chart of the area and what grid to use, but there was ground fog so you couldn't see ahead of you. The *Mackinaw* kept sounding her whistle so we knew where she was."

The three man team searched until their boat ran low on fuel and returned to the *Mackinaw* three hours later.

Peter Hahn

The only survivors were aboard the *Weissenburg*, and Peter Haun said they were trying their best to warm the men back up. "They got some hot tea with a little shot to straighten them out, and the cook had some chicken broth and hot soups to warm them up." Hahn knew that most men could only survive fifteen minutes in the icy water, and he credits his captain with keeping things ready even when Captain Joppich refused help. "We didn't waste any time."

Ed Brewster was amazed at how quickly they were brought aboard the rescue ship. "We got on the life raft and helped other people on and then the Germans come up alongside us. One of the mates from the German ship threw a big line down, he come flying down that line. I never saw such seamanship. He slid down that line and secured the raft, and we all climbed up the jacob's ladder on the German ship."

When the steamer *James Reed* sank in a foggy collision just two decades earlier, survivors gathered in the engine room to warm up. Brewster said the twenty-five *Cedarville* survivors found a tastier place to recover. "We all went into the galley because that was the warmest place of the ship, and they gave us all new clothing."

Gabrysiak said the *Weissenberg's* crew couldn't have been more hospitable. "They asked me, what do you want? I want a cigarette. And I lit one up.. naw, didn't want that. Coffee with a little rum in it.. I thought ahhh.. that warmed me right up, and I took that whole thing, right. Quit shaking right there. Warmed me right up inside."

Peter Hahn says the survivors were so happy that they wanted to pay their rescuers. "They tried to give us money for the rescue,

Len is transferred ashore

but of course you don't do that. Brothers of the sea, you know? Doesn't matter what country you come from, but when you are at sea you need everyone. That's what we did."

The crew was transferred to the cutter *Mackinaw* just after noon, and Bob Bingle was surprised to see his wife when they finally made landfall. "They took us to the Mackinaw City ferry docks. I spotted my wife on the dock, and there were many reporters and I

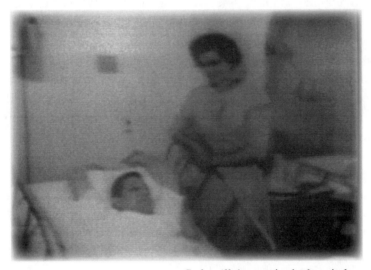

Cedarville's crew in the hospital

jumped in my car and went to the hospital. They told me I would probably be in shock, and they gave me medication that I wouldn't take, but that next morning I was paralyzed. I couldn't walk. It was a week before I could walk."

Gabrysiak spent two days in the Cheboygan hospital nursing his legs with hot packs before he was summoned for a meeting with company officials in Mackinaw City. At 9:30 p.m. he had a knock on his motel door. "They asked me to come down to a room with two or three big lawyers, (Charles) Khoury, the V.P. of U.S. Steel. I wasn't real interested who was there. I should be in the hospital!" Len told the story of what happened and was frustrated by the constant repetition of questions. "I tried to be nice, finally at the

149

end I was getting perturbed. I says, 'I don't know what you're looking for. But you won't find anything different.'"

Gabrysiak was finally able to go back to his room at 1:30 in the morning, and he was instructed to cross the bridge and go to St. Ignace to meet with Coast Guard investigators later in the day. It was here that he saw Captain Joppich again. He remembered the *Cedarville's* master was the first to swear in. "His lawyer said, 'Mr. Joppich is taking the fifth amendment. Who's next in line? Charles Cook. But he's missing yet. Who's next? The wheelsman. Call Mr. Gabrysiak to the stand.'"

Len knew his constitutional right to remain silent, and if it was good enough for his skipper, why not him? "Well I'll take the fifth too.' 'You can't. If you do , we'll subpoena you anyway and you'll have to testify.'"

Gabrysiak figured with all the big lawyers, he was well represented; and the Coast Guard started three hours of questioning for the wheelsman. They offered a break midway through, but he continued on, eager to get home to his wife and son. Gabrysiak returned to the hospital and then came home to Rogers City, but he was far from done with lawyers.

"Couple of days later there was a knock at the door. 'Are you Mr. Gabrysiak? On the *Cedarville?* Yes, I was. Do you have a lawyer? I'd advise you to get one.' And he left. Someone who represented the *Topdalsfjord,* I guess."

Divers descended on the *Cedarville* to not only recover the missing men, but locate crucial logbooks for the investigation. They found the pilothouse logbook, which Gabrysiak said matched his testimony exactly. They also found the bodies of Chief Engineer Donald Lamp, his assistant Reinhold Radtke, wheelsman Bill Assam, steward Wilbert Bredow and Art Furhman, who was trapped below still wearing his heavy weather gear.

The company let the men recover until June, letting a few weeks pass before calling the survivors back to work. Ed Brewster had his fill of sailing. "After I was laid up for about a month and they called me up and said they wanted me to go back to sailing. I said no. I'm not going back."

Bob Bingle had a surprise visit from fellow shipwreck survivor Frank Mays. "He was wondering how things were, what happened. And he helped me overcome it. Told me what to expect. He never did go back sailing himself."

Bob admits the first day back on a ship was tough. All of the men who returned to the fleet were stationed on the *W. F. White*. "When I went aboard it was very hard. I didn't even think I could find the ladder. I stood on deck and could feel the ship rolling. I stood there 20 minutes and didn't think I could do it anymore. I went forward, and down the walkway I could feel the ship rolling over. But once I got up forward I was fine."

Gabrysiak's legs were still giving him trouble when he was asked to come back. He was surprised that the union never offered any sick leave for his time off, and without a paycheck, things were getting tight. "Nobody said anything to me about unemployment, sick pay or nothing. I told Pat, don't worry. I had a couple of endowment policies I took out when I was single. I'll use those if I had to. And that's what I ended up doing."

Nearly a half a year since the sinking, Len was ready for the company to pay up. "Around November I thought what the hell.. we have a contract! We're entitled to some kind of sick pay. I get a hold of the head of the union, called him over to the house. We're entitled to sick pay and all I received was 500 bucks for my lost clothing."

The wheelsman filed a grievance and added up the hours he was entitled to. His union representative returned with a check that was much less than what the wheelsman had predicted. He furiously fired back at the rep, "Don't try to short change me. I don't want any more or any less. I want what I have coming to me. He was back a short while with it."

Gabrysiak was also growing increasingly frustrated with company doctors who couldn't figure out why his leg hurt so bad. He said his manager, Joe Parilla, suggested trying Mercywood Hospital near Ann Arbor. He voluntarily checked in, but soon found that this was more of a sanitarium than an orthopedic recovery center. "The doctors at Mercywood wondered why I wouldn't associate with other people. I told him I had no reason to associate with them. I could see they had rooms below, with bars on them... screaming at night. They tried to keep me doped up. I said 'Keep me locked up, I'm not going anywhere.' Parilla wanted me to go down there and I said I'd agree to that but that's it."

Gabrysiak wouldn't stay cooped up for long. He needed some ointment for psoriasis, and he normally made trips every winter to get the medicine in Ann Arbor. He signed himself out, took a cab

Len Gabrysiak

to the University of Michigan hospital and asked for someone to look at his legs. "Is there anyone I can see while I'm over here and before I go back to Mercywood? And they asked 'how much time do you have?' I said, 'All the time I need. My time is my time while I'm here.'"

In ten minutes he was in with a specialist. "I told him my problem, and raised one leg. 'Put it down. Raise the other leg. Lay on your back.' Raised my legs. I couldn't get up now. What's the story?"

The doctor told Gabrysiak he'd need rehabilitation, starting with weights at least ten times a day. "I said, 'Will you put that in writing?' I was finally getting satisfaction. It was a snap going back to Mercywood, smiling everyday, just waiting for that time."

Nearly two weeks had passed, and Gabrysiak figured it was time to go home. "I got up to the desk and said 'I'm checking out.' His departure was evidently not on the day's agenda, and the unwilling patient boiled over. "I said, 'You let me out of this building now or I may go through that glass window there. And you'll be responsible for anything that happens to me in this place and it's going to be BIG!'"

Gabrysiak said the staff called Parilla and told them of the situation. "I said you tell Mr Parilla my time is up." Gabrysiak was released and returned home to continue his 'recouperation'. That is when he learned that one of the *Bradley* survivors had also been to the company's 'special hospital'. "That's where they put Elmer Fleming after the *Bradley*. Is this because they think it's mental or what? That's what I thought."

Parilla was apparently anxious to see how Gabrysiak's therapy had went downstate. "They said, 'What did you find out in Mercywood?' 'Nothing. I spent time down there for nothing, wasted my time. But I went to University of Michigan and I have a piece of information you may be interested in!'"

Now he had proof that his legs weren't some psychosomatic illness. "I said, 'Number one, you sent me to a place I didn't belong. And number two, and I want you all to hear this, if I would have known the day I walked into here for a job that I would be treated this way, I would have never accepted the job. I would have said stick it.'"

With his injuries, the company couldn't put Gabrysiak back on a ship, so they instead let him wheel a delivery truck. He spent the rest of the winter working as an electrician.

Bob Bingle eventually moved to the *George Sloan*, and by 1998, only two of the *Cedarville* survivors were still sailing the lakes. "Years ago there were a lot of bad nightmares," Bob remembered. In fact, one time I literally threw my wife out of bed. I was just dreaming. Fog never did bother me, and I think of (the accident) every time we go through the straits, go under the bridge, or even on the bridge in a car. That's just the way of life."

The author was honored to make the first documentary to interview the survivors on the *Cedarville*, and wondered if the men had any reservations about exploring the wrecksite with my underwater camera. Bob admitted that he'd like to go along. "It don't bother me that divers are going down there. There's one body left down there. I would like at some point to go down to it... my own curiosity. But I doubt that will happen."

Ed Brewster retired from Proctor and Gamble, and now spends his time with his wife watching their grandkids grow. He started talking publicly about the *Cedarville* in 1997, and frequently volunteers aboard the museum cutter *Mackinaw*.

Captain Joppich lost his license for not following the statutory 'rules of the road' when operating in fog. The Coast Guard found he was going too fast in limited visibility, and judges in the lawsuits criticized his decision to beach the ship with his crew still aboard. The ship steamed for over two miles when it attempted shore, but fell short of its destination by two additional miles.

The course was blamed on the lost third mate, but ultimate responsibility fell on Martin Joppich. Surprisingly, there was little or no blame from his crew. "He was the commander of the ship" Bob Bingle believed, "and he was doing what he felt was right. The other captain was in the same situation. They took equal blame from what I understand as far as court cases. Out in the lake, in the fog, we never ever check down. We run full speed. But I have no hard feelings against the captain."

Peter Hahn said the *Weissenburg's* crew was welcomed as heroes when they finally made port in Cleveland. One reporter asked how he liked America, and he said he'd stay here if he was offered a job. The port of Cleveland hired him that next day, and he retired as the port's general manager thirty-seven years later.

The dangers involved in sailing were even more realized when Bob Bingle was in Ohio for a lawsuit against U.S. Steel. Testifying in a different shipwreck investigation was a man who had just survived thiry-eight hours on a liferaft just like the one that saved Bob's life. The young watchman's name was Dennis Hale, the sole survivor when the *Daniel J. Morrell* broke in half in November, 1966.

Ric's Dive Log

Diving The *Cedarville*

The *Cedarville* is by far the largest shipwreck I've seen intact on the bottom of the Great Lakes, lying in over one hunded feet of water. The forward section is mostly upside down, with a twist at the point of collision that makes the stern more on its starboard side. My first visit was as a beginner diver, exploring the outside of the hull at some forty feet. We went to the pilothouse and filmed the inside, noting that nearly everything was taken out of the room, and only a radar

Cedarville's horn on smokestack- courtesy Mike Kohut

I

156

set hung from what is now the 'ceiling' of the wreck. Those heavy currents that worried wheelsman Len Gabrysiak are certainly worrisome for the diver, and I can attest that they attempt to sweep you right away from

Cedarville's radar

the wreck- and the mooring line that helps you ascend safely.

Visibility is rumored to be as good as fifty feet, but every time I've been there, it's been less than twenty feet. The hull is usually well illuminated by penetrating sunlight, but dark ominous shadows cover the machinery and rails on the top of the decks.

The stern has the most to see, with the streamlined stack reaching sideways into the darkness. Because the ship is at an extreme list, most of the top of the ship is in the shadows. The twin signaling horns are still in place on the smokestack, and it is possible to swim into the stack through an open door. Ventilators and tanks are still in place, as is much of the machinery in the engine room.

The propeller and rudder are not in place, leaving only a prop shaft sticking out where they once powered and steered the ship.

Diver Jim Montcalm on *Cedarville*

157

Cedarville is one of the most popular dive destinations in the straits, located just a few miles from the Mackinac Bridge on the Lake Huron side of the Straits of Mackinac. It lies in the Straits of Mackinac Bottomland Preserve, which provides protection from salvage for over 20 shipwrecks, some of which are over one hundred-fifty years old.

l to r- Ron Raflik, author, Chris Ijames, Frank Mays on *Delta*- Mixter photo

Ric's Dive Log

Diving the *Bradley*

Survivor Frank Mays was one of the first two people to view the
wreck of the *Cedarville* in a submersible, when Expedition '95
tested the *Delta* for a deepwater visit to the *Carl D. Bradley*. Frank
had worked aboard the *Cedarville* before his ill-fated trip on the
Bradley, and the twisted remains of the *Cedarville* were a good
way to get acclimated to searching underwater in the Great Lakes.
We plowed our way to Lake Michigan aboard the rusty barge
Tonawanda, which not only housed the sub and its workshed, but
also quarters for the camera crews and student observers. I use the
term 'quarters' quite loosely, as the below deck accomodations on
the barge were best suited for cargo and not people.

We were not the first people to explore
the *Carl D. Bradley*. The wrecksite,
located near the middle of the lake
between Charlevoix, Michigan, and
Manistique, was previously probed by
U.S. Steel. The owners of the *Bradley*
hired a California crew to observe
the wreck with an underwater camera
mounted on a drill stem. The *Submarex*
found the *Bradley* some 360 feet below
the surface.

Submarex at the Soo

I interviewed former U.S. Steel Great Lakes fleet president Chris
Buekema about his findings, and he was reluctant to talk about it.
He told me it brought up a lot of pain remembering how he had to
notify the victim's families. "The *Bradley* was a hellish period."
Buekema recanted. "You don't get much lower than visiting people
in their living room. I'll never forget the funeral, all those caskets

159

in the gym. It was late November and I'll never forget one woman in Cheboygan telling me how her son used to put the star on the Christmas tree."

Video was in its infancy in 1959, and Beukema only had a black and white monitor to see what the camera captured below. "The visibility was very poor, I thought

Chris Buekema, frmr. U.S. Steel President

it would be clear, but it was very murky and full of sediments. I saw the name and the rudder... and you could see how the deck cracked diagonally."

Newspaper headlines exclaimed the hull was intact, contradicting what the survivors had reported. Buekema was steadfast in telling me that this was correct, full well knowing that we were to visit the wrecksite ourselves in just a few weeks. He remained confident in his assertion that the ship was in one piece. "The thing that has always bothered me is the historians have always talked about how the *Bradley* broke in two pieces. It did not. Had it broke in two, my feeling is that more lives would have been saved because of the buoyancy."

Lawsuits were filed over the seaworthiness of the *Bradley*, and my limited research on the court cases did not turn up whether Beukema's findings were useful in the case. He told me that pictures were taken, but were likely destroyed when the trials were over. I even contacted the law office in New York to try and track down the images, but to no avail.

Lawyers for the families asked for 16 million dollars, and the courts ultimately ordered 1.2 million to the families, which was distributed according to the number of surviving dependents. Attorneys asked for 33 percent of the total settlement, but newspapers reported that Probate Judge Joseph Buza contested their $396,000 fee, saying "In a tragedy like this, everyone loses. No one should profit unduly, despite the great amount of work involved."

Chris Buekema passed away in May of 1999, leaving Mays to get the final word on the mystery of the ship's condition.

The 1995 expedition found that same poor visibility when we dove and expedition leaders scrapped attempts to explore the site after two dives to the shipwreck. Frank Mays was able to see the ship, but only the name on the aft port side. A plaque was left on the wreck, honoring the lost crew and the expedition's attempt at probing the wrecksite. Only a few glimpses of the name, the stack and the stern were brought back to the surface.

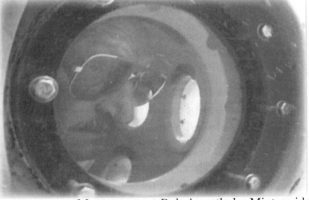

Mays peers out *Delta's* porthole- Mixter video

Mays returned to the *Bradley* two years later, and this time they used an underwater robot rather than risking human lives on the dangerous wreck. I was not part of the crew for this visit, and expedition leaders told reporters that visibility was much clearer and their camera showed the ship "in two separate parts with approximately ninety feet between the forward and aft sections." No proof of their claims was ever released, and despite having sonar capabilities, no scans of the wreckage were shared with the media to verify their claim. I did get to talk with Mays, who was adamant that the ship was separated, verified by sonar measurements underwater.

I have always been puzzled by the claim that the ship was in two pieces. I've interviewed not only Buekema; who admitedly did have a reason to lie about the ship being intact, but also Captain Tom Crawford of the *Submarex*, who didn't have anything to gain by telling me he saw the monitors and noted the hull was intact 'at least on one side.' The Army Corps of Engineers also scanned the site in 1959, noting it was in a crescent moon shape on the bottom, less than 600 feet long. That would certainly indicate the 1997 Expedition was wrong in their measurements. Finally, the testimony of Frank Mays on how the stern sank was also a clue. Mays said the entire stern raised out of the water after the bow had sunk. It just didn't seem possible that a ship full of water would sink in this manner without something pulling it down.

It's interesting to note that zebra mussels have now grown on the wreck, substantially increasing the visibility on the shipwreck. This water clarity was evident when divers removed the ship's bell during the summer of 2007, but the divers never had a chance to investigate the ripped hull.

In 2008, State Police divers scanned the site with hi-resolution sonar. The results show a torn wreck some 570 feet in length, some sixty-feet shorter than the intact ship measured, and clearly shorter than the reported ninety feet of separation. Both the stern and bow are somewhat in-line, indicating they were attached in some way when they sank, and at least one professional observation indicates that the port side is still intact. An uneducated guess is that the bow sank, causing it to pull the stern down as Frank reported, with the propellor blades reaching high above the water as the Bradley slipped beneath the waves. Better scans will indicate why there is a discrepency in the length, but part of that is the fact that the wreck is folded, burying the midsection in the lake bottom with the stern and bow elevated.

162

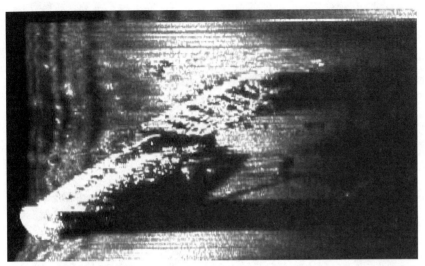

Bradley- courtesy Michigan State Police Underwater Recovery Unit

Learn More About the Wheelsmen!

The incredible stories you've just read were originally
recorded for DVD documentaries. You can hear their amazing
testimonials and find out more about the shipwrecks and storms
in the following videos:

Deep Six: Titanics of the Great Lakes- Featuring the complete
stories on the *Cedarville, Bradley, Morrell* and *Fitzgerald*.

Final Run: Storms of the Century- Ed Kanaby's story along
with profiles and shipwrecks from the 1913 Storm, Gale of
1905, Black Friday 1916, the *Carl D. Bradley*, and the *Daniel J.
Morrell*.

Cutter Rescues- More on the *Escanaba* story along with three
other Coast Guard cutters!

Safe Ashore: The 1940 Armistice Day Storm- The full story
of the *Novadoc*, along with more commentary from wheelsman
Lloyd Belcher and fireman Howard Goldsmith!

www.lakefury.com

Special Acknowledgements

To all the families of the wheelsmen who shared stories, photos and home movies:

Barbara Belcher
Barbara Cross Odstrcil
Sheila Frid
Kelly Ann & Bev Baldwin
Dolly O'Malley
Mike O'Malley
Ben Epstein
The Gabrysiak Family
The Brewster Family
The Bingle Family
Mary Jane Kasprus
Howard Goldsmith

Pictured above
Mary Jane Kasprus, Ed Kanaby's daughter with author

Also special thanks to Peggy Lawrence, who tackled the original manuscript and turned it into something legible. Ron Bloomfield picked up the editor credit from there and taught me a thing or two about punctuation!

The project wouldn't have made it without the help of:

Ralph Roberts
J. Ervin Bates
Brendon Baillod
John Janzen/Inland Sea Corp.
US Coast Guard Historian's Office
Fred Stonehouse
Chuck & Jeri Feltner
Roger LeLievre
Mike Kohut
Steve Harrington
US Steel/Michigan Limestone
Matt Crews
Greg "Capt. Grog" Grieser
David Erickson, Great Lakes Lore
Capt. Bud Robinson
Crew of the *Sundew*
Capt. Harold Muth
Warren Toussaint

Grand Haven Public Library
Sgt. Larry Schloegl, MSP Recovery Unit
Brian Donaldson (Videographer, WNEM)
Ron Raflik (photographer, Expedition '95)
Delta Oceanographics
Eric Jylha

Garry Binecki
Bowling Green University
Jim Reid
Rod Danielson, Rod's Reef Charters
Jeff Wilson
David Trotter
Jeff Moore

Dan Sobeck and family
Richard Wickland

J.C. Carney
National Archives
Frank Mays

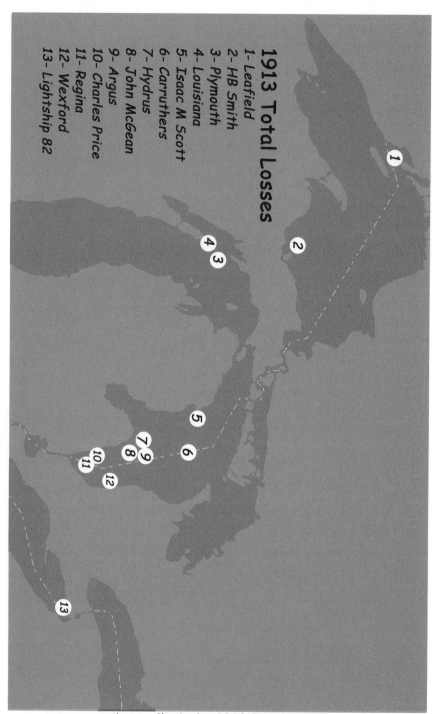

1913 Total Losses

1- Leafield
2- HB Smith
3- Plymouth
4- Louisiana
5- Isaac M Scott
6- Carruthers
7- Hydrus
8- John McGean
9- Argus
10- Charles Price
11- Regina
12- Wexford
13- Lightship 82

Appendix 1 the 1913 Storm

Appendix 11 James Carruthers drawing by Captain Bud Robinson

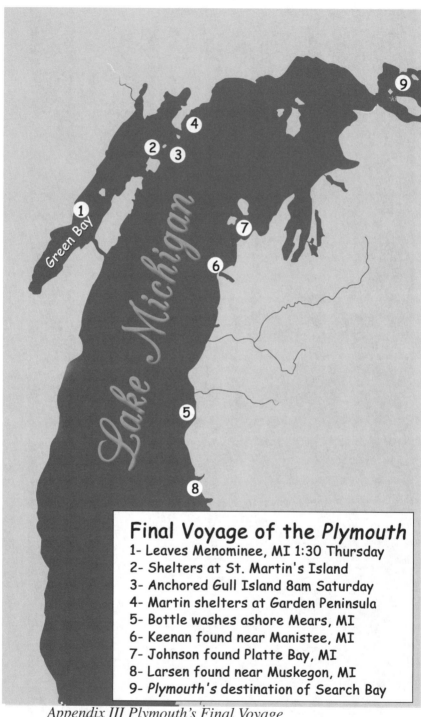

Final Voyage of the *Plymouth*
1- Leaves Menominee, MI 1:30 Thursday
2- Shelters at St. Martin's Island
3- Anchored Gull Island 8am Saturday
4- Martin shelters at Garden Peninsula
5- Bottle washes ashore Mears, MI
6- Keenan found near Manistee, MI
7- Johnson found Platte Bay, MI
8- Larsen found near Muskegon, MI
9- *Plymouth's* destination of Search Bay

Appendix III Plymouth's Final Voyage

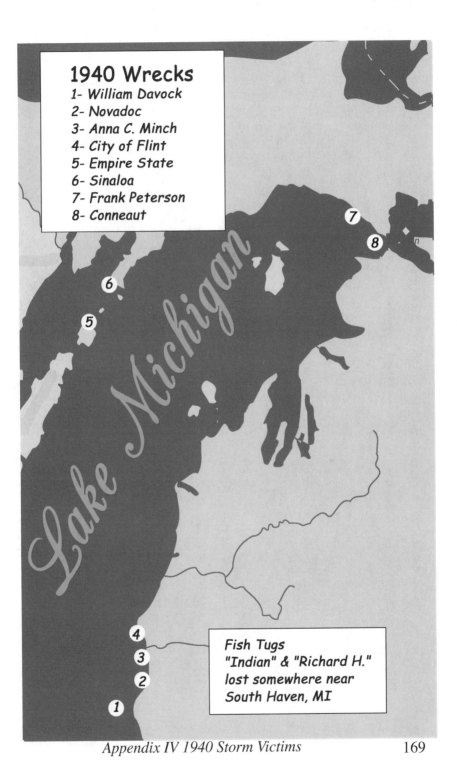

1940 Wrecks
1- William Davock
2- Novadoc
3- Anna C. Minch
4- City of Flint
5- Empire State
6- Sinaloa
7- Frank Peterson
8- Conneaut

Lake Michigan

Fish Tugs
"Indian" & "Richard H."
lost somewhere near
South Haven, MI

Appendix V Telegram to Capt. Cross regarding search for lost crewmen

170

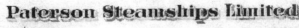

Paterson Steamships Limited

FORT WILLIAM,
CANADA.

November 21st, 1940.

Mr. Clyde Cross,
PENTWATER, Michigan.

Dear Mr. Cross:-

      We wish to take this opportunity
of expressing to you our appreciation for the fine
work done by you and your crew in rescuing the
members of the S.S. "NOVADOC" from their vessel
during the recent disaster. The officers and
representatives of our Company cannot speak too
highly of the very fine job which you did in this
connection and we are enclosing herewith draft in
the amount of $100.00 which we would appreciate if
you would accept from us in this connection.

      Yours very truly,

      PATERSON STEAMSHIPS LIMITED,

      General Manager.

Appendix VI Letter of thanks to Capt. Cross

Ward "M"
Central Division,
Montreal General Hospital.
Dorchester Street, East.
Montreal. P.Q.
Capt. Clyde. A. Cross.   Canada,
Pentwater.   Nov 5th 1941,
Mich.
U.S.A.

My Dear Captain:-

As you will observe I am still a patient in the above hospital, and according to all reports I am likely to be here for some time to come.

I was particularly pleased to learn from the local press, that at long last, you and your men have been publicly recognized by the Canadian Government for your gallant rescue of the Navodoc crew, of which I was a member, and this, almost a year ago.

May I from the depth of my heart, convey to you Sir, and through you to your men, Gustave C. Fisher and Joseph L. Fontaine my eternal gratitude for having saved my life, and I am sure I convey the expressions of the remainder of the saved crew of the Navodoc.

May you long be spared to carry on your chosen profession, and in closing may I ask you to remember me to your charming wife whom I shall never forget, for her unfailing kindness on that unforgettable day Nov 11th 1940

With best regards to you and yours for the coming festive season.

Respectfully and gratefully yours,

John. Petersen.

JP/WBH.   JOHN. PETERSEN.

Appendix VII Letter of thanks to Capt. Cross

MUSIC:
ANNOUNCER: "Back the Attack"

Station WDMJ is pleased to present the only two survivors of the ill-fated Coastguard Cutter Escanaba, in an interview by Earl H. Closser, publicity chairman , Third War Loan Drive. Mr. Closser.

CLOSSER: Good evening. The Coastguard Cutter Escanaba, built at Bay City in 1932, went to war. Proudly she and her crew of 103 men, many of them from the Great Lakes area, carried on her hazardous convoy duties in the Atlantic. Now she lies, broken in two on the bottom of the North Atlantic. Of her gallant crew of 103, only two came back. They are here tonight in this studio./ They didn't want to be here--the 'd rather be back on the firing line. But the Navy department and the U.S. Treasury department knew they had a story to tell-- a story that would bring the war home to the people of the United States. And so Boatswain Mate Melvin Baldwin of Staples, Min ., and Boatswain Mate Raymond F. O'Malley of Chicago are here in the interests of the most important "home front" activity in the history of the nat ion-- the Third War Loan Drive. The public have been told only that the Escanaba sunk as the result of an explosion of undetermined origin. These two men have been told by their superiors that they can tell everything and anything they know. They are not orators-- this interview has been unrehearsed. They are just two American seamen who have gone thru hell and are here to tell you avout it so that you may know how important it is to Back the Attack With War bonds. B aldwin and O'Malley, we're happy to have you here. We hope you are happy to be here too. How about it?

BALDWIN: Yes, we ARE happy to be here. We're happy to be alive and kicking anywhere in these United States.

CLOSSER: And you, Boatswain O'Malley.

O'MALLEY: That goes for me too. I get the shivers when I wake up in the middle of the night thinking "Gosh, it might have been two other fellows making this tour instead of us." That North Atlantic

Appendix VIII Radio Script of Escanaba Sinking WDMJ

water is awful cold and awful deep. Ask us, we know.

CLOSSER: Now, I'm just as curious about a lot of things as all the people listing in tonight. I'm going to fire a lot of questions at you. You don't mind do you?

BALDWIN: No, we don't mind. You see, we can't mind. There's a lot of things we'd rather do than this. There's a lot of things we'd rather think about and talk about than our experiences and the sinking of our ship, but for a little while, before we step back on the new COASTGUARD CUTTER ESCANABA, this is our job-- this is our duty-- and just like millions of other Americans, at home and on the fighting front-- we're doing it whether we like it or not.

CLOSSER: You mentioned the new coastguard cutter Escanaba. What do you mean?

O'MALLEY: A new Coastguard Cutter is now being completed. She will be named the Escanaba. Baldwin and I have been given the chance to serve aboard her. We are to be the first to step aboard.

CLOSSER: Baldwin, I know the Escanaba served on convoy duty for a long time. Won't you tell us about the day by day work of a convoy vessel?

BALDWIN: Well, there isn't much to tell. It's mostly the work of a shepherd dog minding a flock of sheep. The vessels being convoyed zig-zag back and forth, while the destroyers and cutters guarding them and running at a higher rate of speed, zig and zag, out in and out, circle, on the move all the time, ready to dash out after an submarine which may be detected through our sound devices.

CLOSSER: You know the newspapers have printed nothing, until you boys went out on tour, about how the Escanaba was sunk. The accounts merely said that she sank because of an explosion of undetermined origin. Just how did it happen, O'Malley?

OMALLEY: Very simple. We zigged when we should have zagged .

CLOSSER: What do you mean, zigged when we should have zagged?

BALDWIN: He means that we were weaving back and forth as all guarding vessels do, when we ran into the path of a torpedo.

CLOSSER: Aimed at you?

BALDWIN: No, it wasn't. It was aimed at ~~a transport~~, one of the ships we were convoying. We just got in the way.

CLOSSER: How ~~many~~ ships were you convoying?

~~BALDWIN: Two.~~ *I don't know, but it was a small* ~~convoy~~

~~CLOSSER: And how many cutters and destroyers were there?~~

~~BALDWIN: Six.~~

~~CLOSSER: Well, why so many ships to guard just two transports.~~

BALDWIN: Lord Haw Haw, ~~sax~~ in a broadcast from Germany, boasted that the Germans knew all about the two transports and made the boast that they would never reach America. ~~That's the reason for the extra convoy vessels.~~

CLOSSER: Where did the torpedoing take place.

BALDWIN: About ~~half way between Greenland and Newfoundland.~~ *near the east coast of Greenland.*

CLOSSER: Can you tell ~~me~~ us just what took place before and after the sinking.

BALDWIN: No, I can't tell you much about that. I was asleep below. But Boatswain O'Malley was at the helm when it happened.

CLOSSER: O'Malley, maybe you can answer my question.

O'MALLEY: Yes, I was at the helm when it happened. It was on a calm Sunday morning. We had been very active the day and night before chasing down submarine contacts and the crew hadn't had much sleep. The skipper, Lt. Commander Carl Pederson had given orders to let the men sleep as long as they could on that Sunday morning. On the bridge with me were:

Suddenly we had warning through our sound devices that a torpedo was coming toward us from the port side. All the men on the deck ran to that side of the ship to see if they could see it, when, WHAM, it struck us amidships. I ~~saw men falling along the rail~~

The ship lurched and my companions in the wheel
house fell to their knees. I turned to look at them.
One had blood streaming down his face. Another grabbed
my arm and then slipped to the deck, dead. The Officer
of the deck ordered me to get out on the bridge on the
opposite side from where the torpedo struck. I groped
for the door knob. There wasn't any--blown off in the
explosion, I guess. I eyed the porthole. No, that
wasn't big enough to get through. I grabbed a life
jacked and tied it on. Then the men behind me pushed
against me and the door flew open and we burst out
on the bridge. I looked around-- the decks were
torn and shattered--fire ran here and there. Then
the ship broke in two and a wall of water struck me
from behind, sweeping me into the sea. I went down
with the foreward part of the ship but fought my way to
the surface--caught a breath and went down again. Then
the boilers exploded and I was shot to the surface by
its force. The commander Pederson came up right alongside
me. He said :"Make for that floating spar over there"
and we swam over that way." Three men were already
hanging on to it--two were cut and bleeding about the
head and face. The other didn't have a scrath on him--
that was B aldwin. The commander told us to yell as
loud as we could, all together, to attract rescue vessels.
One headed out way, blinking a signal that they had
seen us. Then it swerved off its course. We found out
later it had gotten a submarine contact and had to
take care of that first. It was then, with the rescue
vessel heading off to a different part of the ocean that
I began to feel the piercing chill of the water. it
The temperature, Ixxxxxkxkxxkxkt of the water, I was
later told, was 33 degrees. My hands started to get
numb and I tied myself to the spar with a line that was

Appendix XI Radio Script of Escanaba Sinking WDMJ

One poor fellow hanging on to the spar called for help. But I couldn't help him. I was frozen to it and so numb I couldn't have moved to aid him even if my arm hadn't been frozen tight. On the spar were beside myself, two officer, one the commander, a seaman and Boatswain O'Malley. Sometime after I lost consciousness, all but O'Malley and me slipped beneath the water, never to be seen again.

CLOSSER: What happened when you regained consciousness aboard the rescue vessel?

BALDWIN
O'MALLEY: I asked one of the fellows how they made out picking up the rest of the crew. He said if I'd turn my head a little I'd see the rest of the crew that had been saved. I thought to myself, "Well, they must have done all right picking up the men". So I turned my head and there was the rest of the crew all right. It was O'Malley.

CLOSSER: You told me this morning that you were present at the invasion by American troops of Africa. That's right, isn't it? O'Malley?

O'MALLEY: Yes, that's right. We were on another cutter then. I was assigned as coxwain, at the helm of an invasion barge carrying tanks and troops from the tramsports to the shore. Most people back here think that the African landing was easy. Well, it wasn't so easy. It took us 72 hours to establish the beach head. It isn't just a matter of piling into a small boat, start up the motor and go to shore.

My barge was in the first wave that started out for shore. Part way to shore it was shot out from under me. The soldiers had full field packs on and when they jumped in or were thrown into the water, they became a little nervous. Some of them called for help as they were drowning. Others were hit as they struggled in the water by shells from the shore batteries.

One poor fellow hanging on to the spar called for help. But I couldn't help him. I was frozen to it and so numb I couldn't have moved to aid him even if my arm hadn't been frozen tight. On the spar were beside myself, two officer, one the commander, a seaman and Boatswain O'Malley. Sometime after I lost consciousness, all but O'Malley and me slipped beneath the water, never to be seen again.

CLOSSER: What happened when you regained consciousness aboard the rescue vessell?

BALDWIN
O'MALLEY: I asked one of the fellows how they made out picking up the rest of the crew. He said if I'd turn my head a little I'd see the rest of the crew that had been saved. I thought to myself, "Well, they must have done all right picking up the men". So I turned my head and there was the rest of the crew all right. It was O'Malley.

CLOSSER: You told me this morning that you were present at the invasion by American troops of Africa. That's right, isn't it? O'Malley?

O'MALLEY: Yes, that's right. We were on another cutter then. I was assigned as coxwain, at the helm of an invasion barge carrying tanks and troops from the transports to the shore. Most people back here think that the African landing was easy. Well, it wasn't so easy. It took us 72 hours to establish the beach head. It isn't just a matter of piling into a small boat, start up the motor and go to shore.

My barge was in the first wave that started out for shore. Part way to shore it was shot out from under me. The soldiers had full field packs on and when they jumped in or were thrown into the water, they became a little nervous. Some of them called for help as they were drowning. Others were hit as they struggled in the water by shells from the shore batteries.

I started to swim toward the anakaxx transport and was
picked up by the first barge that came along. It wouldn't
stop for you--it couldn't. It's job was to get men ashore
as fast as it could. But if you could grab ahold of it
as it went by or someone aboard grabbed your hand and gave
you a lift, it was all right. When we got back to the
ship, I was ordered into another barge, loaded with a
tank and infantrymen. I got that barge ashore. The tank
rolled off on the beach, with the infantrymen leaping off
to follow behind it. As it went up on the beach, it struck
a land mine and was blown to bits. The infantrymen running
behind got the full force of the explosion. Some had their
faces kizmuxafixxthaxxstorn off. Others were killed by the
concussion. Just then I saw something flying through the air
toward me. I ducked and it landed on the deck of the barge.
I looked down. It was a man's hand. Then I looked to the
beach. There stood a soldier--dumfounded--looking at
the torn stump of his axm wrist. He then slumped to the
ground. Whether he fainted or died, I don't know.

On another trip to shore with a barge, an enemy plane
dove on is, with machine gun bullets spraying all around us.
The infantrymen jumped overboard and started toward shore.
One was hit by four machine gun slugs, one in each wrist
and one in each leg. He dropped. A buddy offered to help
him to shore. He said, "No go on, I'll take care of myself."

Those are some of the things the boys on the fighting
fronts are going through. They are doing their best. They
have to or lose their lives. They have to kill or be
killed.

All I can do for the boys over there is to urge you
to Buy War Bonds, and more War bonds-- to urge you to
invest in the U.S.A,, the best country in theworld, and at
the same time put a gun into the hands of an American boy
fighting for his country. When you do that you may save

the life of some soldier who is fighting to keep the
United States a free country.

CLOSSER: Baldwin, were you on the african invasion.

BALDWIN: Yes, but I was aboard the cutter all the time, firing at
shore batteries and helping to transport the wounded.

CLOSSER: I know that you are out on this tour to bring home to the
people of Marquette county the great need for us to
Back the Attack With War Bonds. What do you, and the other
boys out on the fighting fronts, feel about this Third
War Loan Drive?

BALDWIN: (Make same appeal as at Delft theater this afternoon)

CLOSSER: Thank you, Boatswain O(Malley and Boatswain Baldwin. You
have brought the war and its horrors closer home to us . When
you get back into action again, tell your buddies that
Marquette county is backing and will continue to back your
attack with bonds and more bonds. Thank And now, the Third
War Loan Drive theme song, "Back the Attack".

USS ESCANABA LOST CREWMEN
OFFICERS:
Lieutenant Commander Carl Uno Peterson
Lieutenant Robert Henry Prause, Jr.
Lieutenant John N.C. Hunt
Lieutenant (j.g.) James Sullivan (R)
Lieutenant (j.g.) William Perley Thoman
Lieutenant (j.g.) Jesse Carter Treadwell (R)
Ensign Richard Andrea Arrighi (R)
Ensign Daniel Cornelius Davis (R)
Ensign John David Cameron, Jr. (R)
Ensign William Cline Garcia (R)
Ensign Robert E. McGehearty (R)
Ensign Woodrow Wilson Wilkins (R)
Assistant Surgeon Ralph Robert Nix, USPHS

ENLISTED CREW:
ALSTON, John; RM3c (R)
ANDERSON, Ralph Ashford; SM2c (R)
ARIDAS, George; Sea1c (R)
BATHS, William; Y2c (R)
BAUER, Norman Michael Donald; WT2c
BIGGS, Melvin Gear; Sea 2c (R)
BONHAM, Max Anderson; MM1c
BROWN, Oren Ernest; SOM3c (R)
BUDDENHAGEN, Ray Herbert; MM2c (R)
BUKES, Ted Speros; RM3c
BURNS, Thomas Francis; SM2c (R)
BYKOWSKI, Raymond Joseph; Cox
CARD, James Freeman; F2c (R)
CHRISTENSON, Clarence Edwin; BM2c
CHAPLEAU, Eugene; Sea1c (R)
CHAPMAN, Lyle Thomas; Sea1c
CHUDACOFF, Sam Y3c (R)
CILO, John, Jr.; MM2c (R)
CLARK, Alfred Eldon; MM2c (R)
CLARK, Herman Reginald; SOM2c

COREY, William Horace; GM1c
COUNSELOR, Layton Richard; CMM (a)
CZELUSNIAK, George Joseph; Sea1c (R)
DAVIS, James Francis, Jr.; C. Y. (a) (R)
DELSART, Leonard; RM1c
DEYAMPERT, Warren Traveous; Off. Std. 2c
DODGEN, Paul Chapman; QM3c
ESTOCAPIO, Pedro Abenoja; Off. Std. 2c
FARRAR, Clarence Albert; CMM (a)
FERRIS, Donald Edward; WT2c
FOSTER, Charles Robert; RM2c
GADEK, Eugene; RM1c
GATOS, Lloyd James; F1c
GMEINER, George Walter; Sea 1c (R)
GRAHAM, Leroy J. Allen; SOM2c
HAWK, Arthur Lloyd; Sea 2c (R)
HOOPER, Frank Van; EM2c
HOSTAK, Quirin; Sea 1c (R)
JAROUSKY, Phillip; WT1c
JOHNS, Floyd Raymond; Sea 2c (R)
KENNY, Joseph Paul; Sea 1c (R)
KLETZIEN, Kenneth Albert; SOM2c
KUCIA, Edward John; WT2c
KURCZ, Stanley Joseph; RM1c
LARSON, George Wilfred; CBM (a)
LAYTON, Clyde; CBM (a)
LIETZ, Ralph Frederic; Sea 1c1c
LOBOSCO, Angelo Frank; Sea 1c (R)
LONDO, Victor Joseph Jr.; UT1c
LUCAS, Joseph William; SC1c
McCARTHY, Barton; GM3c
McCREADY, Robert Garr; SM2c (R)
McGOWAN, Ralph; Sea 1c (R)
MENKOL, Theodore Thomas; GM2c
MEYERS, John Benjamin; SC2c
MICKLE, Charles Ray; CWT
MOHLER, Malcolm Eroy; WT2c

Escanaba Crew Listing XVII

MORE, Sidney Albert; SOM3c
NEALE, Arthur Frederick; RM3c (R)
NILSEN, Roy; Sea 1c (R)
NOWAKOWSKI, Bronislaw; Sea 1c
O'LEARY, Walter Francis; Sea 1c (R)
PALSER, Hugh; QM1c
PAOLELLA, Valentino Natale; Sea 1c (R)
PETERSON, Leo Rudolph; Cox (R)
REDNOUR, Forrest Oren; SC2c
RICE, James Joseph; SK2c (R)
ROWLAND, Robert Hall; SOM3c
RUIDL, Patrick Carl; RDM3c
SALM, Victor Nicholas CM3c (R)
SALTER, Claud Alexander; CBM
SATTLER, Kenneth Eldon; RM1c
SICKLES, Frank Ernest Jr.; Sea 1c (R)
SKARIN, Clifford Burton; Y2c (R)
SMITH, Clayton Robert; Sea 1c
SOMES, Thomas Bennett; QM1c
SOMMERS, Joseph Charles; Sea 1c (R)
SWANDER, Dwight Earl; RM2c
TESCHENDORF, Leo Leroy; CMM (a)
TIERNEY, William Charles; Ph. M. 2c (R)
TILLETT, Thomas; M. Att. 2c (R)
TYRUS, Earl James; M. Att. 2c (R)
WELSH, Dean Marvin ;CM1c
WESTMORE, Edward Valentine Tait, Jr.; F2c (R)
WIDMAN Axel Victor Waldemar; RDM 3c (R)
WILLIAMS, Samuel, Jr.; M. Att.1c
YORK, Clyde Bradley; MM1c
YURIK, Victor; F2c
(source US Coast Guard Historians Office)
notations:
USPHS: U.S. Public Health Service
(R): Coast Guard Reserve
(a): Acting

Escanaba Crew Listing XVIII

		181	172	30.62	40	SSE	5	O,R	NS	10	6	7	Anm.		
		141	173	30.63	40	SSE	5	O,R	NS	10	6	4	Vacancy		
		139	173	30.64	38	SSE	5	O,R	NS	10	6	4	Extra No.	1	7
		139	173	30.65	36	SSE	5	O,R	NS	10	6	4	General mess rations issued	73	
		128	173	30.66	36	SSE	5	O,R	NS	10	6	4	Commuted rations issued	1	1

Temp.: Max. 48 Min. 48 Drills held: General Quarters, Artificial Resuscitation

RECORD OF THE MISCELLANEOUS EVENTS OF THE DAY

Midnight to 4:00 p.m.

Underway on course 183°T various speeds in company with S.S. Fairfax, U.S.S. Escanaba, U.S.S. Storis, U.S.S. Laramie, U.S.S. Algonquin, U.S.S. Tampa, and U.S.S. Mojave, enroute to Argentia, Newfoundland.

H.C. Brush, Ens.

4:00 a.m. to 8:00 a.m.
Sounded General Quarters.

Underway as before. 0510 U.S.S. Escanaba sunk, position 60-40 North, 52-10 West. 0600 Picked up BALDWIN, Melvin A. 225-296) BM.2/c., O'MALLEY, Raymond F. (203-867) Sea 1/c; survivors U.S.S. Escanaba. 0620 Picked up LIEUT. ROBERT H. PRAUSE, U.S.C.G.; Executive Officer, U.S.S. Escanaba. 0700 Secured from search for Survivors. Underway as course 183°T, variable speed in company with U.S.S. Storis.

8:00 a.m. to noon.
Underway as before. 10:30 Artificial resuscitation failed to revive Lieut. ROBERT H. PRAUSE; considered dead.

12:00 noon to 4:00 p.m.
Underway as before.

H.C. Brush, Ens.

4:00 p.m. to 8:00 p.m.
Underway as before. 4:15 Changed course to 173°T

8:00 p.m. to midnight
Underway as before.

Approved for the day:

H.B. Roussan

Examined and found to be complete:

H.C. Brush

184   *Appendix XIX:* Tug *Raritan* Logbook June 13, 1943

3		211	180	31.08	45	N	2	O,R	N6	10	4	6
7		211	176	31.08	43	NNE	2	O	N6	10	4	6
8		211	176	31.06	41	NNE	3	O	N6	10	4	5
9		210	176	31.03	40	NNE	3	O,R	N6	10	4	4
0		210	176	31.03	39	NE	3	O,R	N6	10	4	4
1		211	176	31.03	38	NE	3	O,R	N6	10	4	4
2		213	176	31.02	38	NE	3	O,R	N6	10	4	4

AWL.
Ah.
Ahm.
Vacancy.
Extra No. _1_ _9_
General mess rations issued. _25_
Commuted rations issued. _1_ _1_

ag. Temp.: Max. **46** Min. **44** Drills held:

RECORD OF THE MISCELLANEOUS EVENTS OF THE DAY

Midnight to 4:00 a.m.

Underway on course 173° T, variable speeds, in
company with U.S.S. Storis, enroute to Argentia,
Newfoundland.

H.C. Brush, Ens.

4:00 a.m. to 8:00 a.m.

Underway as before.

8:00 a.m. to 12:00 noon.

Underway as before. 0805 changed course to 180° T.
0930 Buried Lieut. Robert H. Prause, U.S.C.G., Executive Officer
U.S.S. Escanaba, at sea, approx. position 58 N, 52 W
with appropriate honors.

12:00 noon to 4:00 p.m.

Underway as before. Approximate speed 45 knots.

H.C. Brush, Ens.

4:00 p.m. to 8:00 p.m.

Underway as before. 6:24 Changed course to 176° T.

8:00 p.m. to midnight.

Underway as before.

Examined and found to be complete:

Appendix XX Tug *Raritan* Logbook June 14, 1943   185

Davock Crew List
Missing:
Captain Charles "Billy" Allen
Andrew Stiffler, Wheelsman
Joseph Rokowski, Watchman
James Gordan, Deckwatchman
Woodring Wilson, Deckhand
John T Burns, Chief Engineer
Jere Collins, First Assistant
Engineer
Harold Mullen, Second Assis-
tant Engineer
Arnold Johnson, Third Assis-
tant Engineer
Carl Sharraw, Oiler
Charles Findlay, Oiler
Jay Wezer, Oiler
Frank Parker, Fireman
Lyle Doyle, Fireman
Charles Ferguson, Fireman
Orville Shurkey, Coal Passer
Godfree Lietka, Coal Passer
Homer Youkins, Coal Passer
Laurence Gonyea, Steward
Lyle Campbell, Second Cook
John Janatis, Porter
Charles Flint, Porter

Deceased crew:
Charles Price, First Mate
John Wiesen, Second Mate
Leroy Shurkey, Third Mate
Frank Stonek, Wheelsman
Walter Kiewice, Wheelsman
James Bowman, Watchman
Edward Becker, Deckwatchman
James Saunders, Deckhand

186   *Appendix XXI*

Novadoc Crew List

Survivors:

Captain Donald Steip
Richard Simpell, First Mate
Alaric Blanchette, Second Mate
Lloyd Belcher, Wheelsman
Bill Morrison, Wheelsman
Joe Lacasse, Lookout
Douglas Houden, Lookout
Ernie Lalonde, Chief Engineer
Fred Chessels, Second Engineer
Clifford Goldsmith, Oiler
Dave Prentiss, Oiler
Howard Goldsmith, Fireman
John Peterson, Fireman
James Quinn, Fireman
Everett Turner, Deckhand
Tom Robinson, Seaman
Ray King, Seaman

Missing:
Joseph DeShaw, Steward
Phillip Flavin, Second Steward

Appendix XXII

Anna C. Minch Crew List

Missing Crew (As of the Canadian Investigation):
Captain Donald A Kennedy
Russell Elyea, First Mate
Howard Kirton, Steward
Mabel Kirton, Assistant Steward
William Vollick, Wheelsman
Charles Myers, Fireman
Stanley McNabb, Fireman
Dan Rose, Fireman
Howard Contois, Fireman
Martin Dillon, Oiler
James MacEachern, Oiler
Robert Vollick, Ordinary Seaman
Russell Thompson, Ordinary Seaman
Irvin Galliano, Ordinary Seaman
Vincent Reive, Chief Engineer
James Barker, Second Engineer

Deceased:
Gordan Jeffrey, Second Mate
Lawrence Thompson, Wheelsman
George Sovey, Lookout
Sheldon MacMath, Lookout
Clifford Contois, Ordinary Seaman

Appendix XXIII

Cedarville Crew List

Survivors:
Capt. Martin Joppich
Leonard Gabrysiak, Wheelsman
Angus Domke, Watchman
Ivan Trafelet, Watchman
Edward Brewster, Watchman
Robert Bingle, Deckwatchman
Larry Richard, Deckhand
Elmer Emke, Deckhand
Harry Bey, Second Assistant Engineer
Michael Idalski, Third Assistant Engineer
William Friedhoff, Oiler
Billy Holley, Stokerman
Anthony Rosmys, Stokerman
Arthur Martin, Second Cook
David Erickson, Porter

Deceased:

Donald Lamp, Chief Engineer
Reinhold Radtke, Third Assistant Engineer
Wilbert Bredow, Chief Steward
William Asam, Wheelsman
Arthur Fuhrman, Deckwatchman
Edward Jungman, Deckwatchman
Stanley Haske, Wheelsman

Missing Crewmen (as of Coast Guard Investigation):
Charles Cook, Third Mate
Eugene Jones, Stokerman
Hugh Wingo, Oiler

Bradley Crew List

Survivors:
Elmer Fleming, First Mate
Frank Mays, Watchman

Deceased:
Carl Bartell
Alfred Boehmer
Richard Book
Alva Budnick
William Elliott
Erhardt Felax
Cleland Gager
Paul Heller
Paul Horn
Raymond Kowalski
Joseph Krawczak
Alfred Pilarski
Gary Price
Leo Promo, Jr.
Bernard Schefke
Gary Strzelecki
Edward Vallee
John Zoho

Missing (as of Coast Guard Report)
Douglas Bellmore
Capt. Roland Bryan
John Fogelsonger
Raymond Buehler
Clyde Enos
John Bauers

Index

*(**bold** indicates photos)*

About the Author:

Ric grew up as the oldest of seven Mixter children living in a
house trailer in Sands, Michigan. His love for history was immediately apparent when he learned to write Phoenician in high school,
but his work as a historian would only emerge after several years
as a television reporter.

His interest in shipwrecks occurred when the gasoline tanker
Jupiter exploded only a few miles from his house. Sent 'on-scene'
as a cameraman, he spent several days covering the disaster, including a walk on its melted decks a week later.

SCUBA certified only a few months later, Ric would borrow an
underwater video camera to observe his first submerged ship.
The results were an "Excellence in Broadcasting" award with the
Michigan Association of Broadcasters in 1991.

Since then, Ric has visited over 100 shipwrecks, including a dive
to the *Edmund Fitzgerald* in 1994. He has donated nearly 40 TV
shows to PBS and also appeared as a shipwreck researcher for the
History Channel and Discovery Networks. He is a frequent lec-
turer at symposiums around the Great Lakes and has shared his
underwater adventures with museums in Michigan, Minnesota,
Wisconsin and Ohio. In 2009, the Association for Great Lakes
Maritime History awarded Ric for sharing decades of shipwreck
stories with the world.

Ric is also a pilot, flying missions in military and civilian aircraft
that include biplanes, B-52s, an F-16, the Goodyear Blimp and
countless others. His company, Airworthy Productions, reflects his
love for flying which is only rivaled by his passion for diving.

Ric has three children and lives with his wife Sheila in Michigan.

Mixter Documentary Chronology:

Best Adventure Yet (1992)

The 1913 Storm (1993)

Expedition 94 to the Edmund Fitzgerald (1994)

The Ship Time Forgot (Series on the Bradley (1995)

The Edmund Fitzgerald Investigation (1997)

Deep Six (1998)

Great Lakes Indepth- Episodes 1-26 (2000-01)

Safe Ashore (2003)

Final Run (2004)

Cutter Rescues (2006)

Bombs Away (2008)

The Edmund Fitzgerald Investigations (2008)

Cement Boat (2009)

Offshore Outposts (2011)

Sunken Treasure (2012)